T0103758

My World with *Rafiki*

An Economic Travelogue and Miscellany

BISWAJIT NAG

PARTRIDGE

A Penguin Random House Company

Copyright © 2014 by Biswajit Nag.

ISBN:	Softcover	978-1-4828-3673-8
	eBook	978-1-4828-3672-1

All rights reserved. No part of this book may be used or reproduced by any means, graphic, electronic, or mechanical, including photocopying, recording, taping or by any information storage retrieval system without the written permission of the publisher except in the case of brief quotations embodied in critical articles and reviews.

Because of the dynamic nature of the Internet, any web addresses or links contained in this book may have changed since publication and may no longer be valid. The views expressed in this work are solely those of the author and do not necessarily reflect the views of the publisher, and the publisher hereby disclaims any responsibility for them.

To order additional copies of this book, contact
Partridge India
000 800 10062 62
orders.india@partridgepublishing.com

www.partridgepublishing.com/india

To
my students
and Little Bornik
(who loves stories)

Preface

I travelled to Kerala for the first time to attend a conference on 500 years of India–Europe relations in the late 1990s. This was to commemorate the arrival of Vasco da Gama in India. Conference authority was kind enough to support a doctoral student with AC-II tier train fare in mid of May. I decided to extend my stay for a couple of days more to visit Kanyakumari (Cape Comorin), especially the sunrise which I was told not to miss. As there was no reservation available, I bought a waiting list ticket in a night train along with a lecturer from a Delhi college. While the train reached Cochin at midnight, we discovered that no way our tickets would get confirmed. We ran towards the general unreserved compartment and found it almost impossible to get into. Somebody pushed me from the back, and I fell straight inside the train. It was almost dark as there were only few dim lights that illuminated the compartment partially. There were at least 150–200 people inside the compartment, and most of them were sitting on the floor and dozing. I fell on the lap of an old man who expressed his anger with a couple of words uttered in Malayalam language and then started snoring badly. I tried to adjust myself in the darkness and got a place to stand. Fortunately, I could lean on the wall. The train started to move, and soon I also fell asleep. Around 4 a.m. we reached our destination. I got off with severe back pain. Thousands of people disembarked from the train and all were walking slowly without any noise or commotion. Living in North India for more than a decade, this was a surprise to me. I was habituated to see usual fights at the New Delhi railway station and involvement of police every time in front of the unreserved compartment of a long distance train especially going to Uttar Pradesh and Bihar. Four hours frictionless night train journey without even a seat in a general compartment was unimaginable in the northern part of the country.

A country can be completely different from one part to the other in terms of culture, tradition, and practices. Our hapless economic theories made umpteenth attempts to model human behaviour to understand the policy implication on the society. However, priorities, perception, and practices are different from one group to another (even among individuals) and so is the impact of development policies. Sociologists, anthropologists, and even historians have provided enough food for thought on this. Still, when you experience the difference on your own, you tend to provide a new dimension, a complete new hypothesis, maybe a new prognosis. Perhaps, the seed for writing this book was germinated due to this drive. I had the habits in my childhood to write the names of the railway stations when we were travelling a long distance. I showed it (the list of stations from Bhopal to Jabalpur) once to my geography teacher as part of my summer-holiday homework. He politely advised me to write a few paragraphs. I took help from my parents to get more information about Madhya Pradesh, especially dresses, food habits, and festivals, and wrote a small essay in my school magazine (my first literary work). Today, while I am writing the preface of this book, I feel that I have been preparing for this book for many decades.

I was hearing Prof. Vijay Mahajan about marketing issues in India. He cleverly divided the Indian market into four regions: south, very loyal; west, price conscious; east, believes in tradition; and north, loves to experiment. These brilliant yet very general groupings can easily entice researchers to go further down to discover the reasons behind such behavioural differences. For any new company in India, it is a Herculean task to understand Indian culture and consumer behaviour. Several companies have started sending their employees to do a short course on business administration in India and learn Hindi. For global managers, knowledge of history, contemporary politics, and cultural issues are now essential along with their ability to grasp economic and business policies. Indian companies have also now started to venture outside. Many of such companies consider international business as an extension of Indian business and thereby limit themselves to export and import only with some amount of investment for streamlining distributional channels and manage promotional activities. However, as international business grows, companies feel the cost pressure and pressure of local responsiveness in foreign market.

At this juncture, companies need to ensure a consistent international strategy corresponding to the nature of foreign market based on existing status of the economy, political stability, business environment, and consumer behaviour.

Teaching subjects which are offshoots of economics, such as world economy or global business environment, in B-school is quite challenging as students are from varied backgrounds with rich practical experiences. On top of it, for people like us who are trained in formal economics, it's a double trouble. We try to preach with unrealistic assumptions to make the idea simple and sometimes so simple which is far from reality. All teachers then take the recourse of case studies to make the theories believable. In a postgraduate class of economics, the nuts and bolts of theories themselves generate sufficient interest, and students may elevate themselves to another plain with changing assumptions and extending the ideas. The excitement of remaining in the world of theories is the main driving force to the development of the subject, but when students are from different backgrounds and interested about the interdisciplinary world, it is a compulsion for teachers to steer the classroom discussion to that direction. For years, I have been doing this or, in other words, running between Scylla and Charybdis to explain trade theories in one side and growth of world business in the post-war period, rise of China, and fall of USSR on the other side, along with firm level strategic choice in different business environments.

The genesis of the book is rooted to the classroom discussion on various issues pertaining to conducting business internationally. While teaching I tend to link and share useful experiences along with the lecture notes. These examples were enriched by more introspection through the follow-up discussions. This book is an attempt to write an economic travelogue intermixing my lecture notes and travel experience. The Western world has made an attempt to capture everything through systems and structure; hence, people find a large similarity in developed worlds in terms of business culture, procedures, and the style in economic management. However, the developing world is widely different as their history and evolution are diverse. With the slowing down of developed economies, our urge to understand the modernisation effort of developing countries have increased by many folds. Professors from developed country universities are running around the world and trying to construct meaningful case studies on the social experiment happening everywhere and their impact on business and economy. This book is a collection of such examples from India's perspective, or in other words, it depicts how India or Indians look at the world as our country is increasingly getting integrated with the rest of the world. It is due to the insistence of my students that I have decided to now put them in documented form. The final product has moved away from economic travelogue and become more a miscellany related to contemporary socio-economic paradigm. *Rafiki* means 'friend' in Kiswahili language, which is spoken in a large part of Africa. The main message in the book is 'Knowing a country means knowing the people and making friends'. It highlights the importance of cooperation and co-creation with friendly nations for mutual prosperity. The book describes the role of history, culture, religion, corruption, politics, etc. in economic policymaking especially in the contemporary developing world, including India. It is full of anecdotal evidences linked with policies and practices pursued by countries. I made an attempt to break the standard practice by bringing a narrative mode in writing style to reach a wider audience. The book, especially the conclusion chapter, can be used more as a tool for teachers and students to analyse the international business environment. It can as well be treated as casual non-fiction. Nonetheless, the ideas are highly opinion based; hence, readers may have an opposite view. The objective of the book is to persuade readers to have a critical appreciation of economic and social issues with their own logic.

Acknowldgements

From a daily life of lecturing, publishing journal articles, advising the government and corporate sector, it was an enthusiasm as well as trepidation to take up this project. Any book, especially the first one, does not come into existence without a lot of assistance and help. This book would not see the light without those people who are described in the chapters. I thank all of them for sharing their experiences with me at various points of time. I am grateful for the lessons I learnt from them. I also would like to thank individuals and organizations who have given me permission to use their data and refer to research works conducted by them.

Without the advice and support of those who are in my daily contact, this book would not be completed. Let me begin with Pinaki, Debashis, and Triptendu with whom I shared my ideas in details. Their close scrutiny and encouragement kept me going since the last one and a half year. My companionship with Pinaki at IIFT in the last fourteen years probably spells everything. Close to me as a colleague and friend, his contribution in this book was colossal. The idea of making IIFT a place for interdisciplinary and lateral learning has been encouraged by him and his support to operationalize this through various courses was remarkable. This theme has seamlessly flown into the chapters of this book. From the days of brewing thoughts to finalization of the manuscript, his enquiry and critical views pushed me to think differently and rewrite several chapters in a different way. I have derived many ideas, especially how to use anecdotes, from Debashis who has taught me to see the world through the writings of great people. Triptendu, being a bohemian, has given his views at the initial stage, linking Takla Makan with Timbuktu. That was a brilliant idea to see things from a different angle, and he forced me to study history and politics more before I jumped into writing. Some of my other colleagues, such as Anil, Bibek, Bimal, Jaydeep, and Vineet, I took for granted, yet their help in developing ideas was precious. My sincere thanks go to Girish and Chanchal; without their typing help, this book would not have come up so easily. Ann Minoza and Marie Giles have provided excellent editorial support with diligence and patience. It was pleasure working with them.

Students, my precious assets, have significant contribution in this project. I have organized my thoughts through their eyes. Their relentless questions in the late evening class or at hostel mess provided lots of inputs and guided my research on the topics. Discussions with former students, whether at a midnight café in Accra or during an afternoon walk at Saarbrücken or in a friendly dinner at Dar or maybe a chat at Fremantle railway station, are not only nostalgic but important too. I received lots of valuable information about their business and, in many cases, unearthed new policy barriers which otherwise I would not have come across. This book is dedicated to all my students.

My son, Bornik, has been a little more curious seeing me working on a 'storybook' lately. Little he understands economics and management, his interest on stories is invaluable for me. He has contributed in finalizing the cover page revealing his version of how to make a better world. As he loves stories, this book is dedicated to him also for his future reading.

My wife, Bansari, has also burnt the midnight lamp giving her critical comments on chapters for final positioning of the book. Several ideas I discussed with her from time to time, and she helped me put them in a thread. Other than her, it was almost impossible to complete the final chapters.

My mother is a little more anxious as she is not getting regular calls from me since the last couple of weeks. Of late, she is also curious to know how I am going to wind up the book. Being an avid reader, she has provided her intelligent observation on the writing style. Her incessant love and warm appreciation as I took each step ahead has augmented my interest to complete this work.

While I am submitting this manuscript to the publisher, I would like to sincerely apologise if I have hurt anyone unintentionally through my writings. Though the book embodies the help and influences of many, I pen-off being solely responsible for all errors and mistakes. The views expressed are entirely mine and don't belong to the people mentioned in the book.

Travel is fatal to prejudice, bigotry, and narrow-mindedness.

Mark Twain

Contents

List of Tables

List of Figures

1

Brand Value: Do Economists Understand Marketing Jargon?

As a student of economics, we were never exposed to the nitty-gritty of subjects like marketing, finance, HR, etc. as our subjects mostly deal with economic fundamentals. Sometimes they become difficult to apply in real-life situations due to their rigid assumptions and simplicity (or complexity). While teaching in a B-school, this was my first hurdle to explain economic theories to students who have varied backgrounds with very rich experiences. Teaching economics here requires good communication skill and ability to connect with practical examples. Books are always full of such nice cases but the teacher's own experience matters a lot. This not only gives confidence to a teacher but students can also understand and appreciate economic theories, relating them to other applied subjects such as marketing. Often, we face questions related to other subjects, and students expect that economics, being the mother of all management subjects, has an answer.

One such topic which baffled me is about the concept of brand value. When students ask such questions, we tend to give a reply which is mostly philosophical, trying to understand the value of a commodity or a product. In mid 1990s, I had an an experience which was an eye-opener to me regarding brand value. It was below the Eiffel Tower in Paris when a vendor was persuading me to buy some mementos. I was a mere doctoral student (cash-strapped)

1

and on a short trip to attend a conference hosted by the European Union. The conference authority was kind enough to provide me some per diem and a week-long ticket for the Paris Metro. I crisscrossed the city and visited numerous museums, popular spots, and tried to discover the city on my own way (just like the real backpacker). After more persuading, when the vendor felt that it was hard to sell, he yelled, 'Why don't you buy this balloon? You can carry the air of Paris.' He was serious though I gave him a surprised look. 'I mean it. You can take this (air of Paris) just paying few francs.' A balloon for a few francs. I was converting how many rupees I had to pay to buy a balloon. 'Hmmm, it is quite costly to buy the brand Paris even hidden in a balloon.' So what is the value of the air inside the balloon or the balloon itself? We cannot disassociate the products in this way. This is a complete package. We know that air comes free to every individual, but the air of Paris or New York have different interpretations. This concept of branding out of nothing has given the shock of how you calculate the value of a product or service.

In 2007, *Washington Post* did a social experiment with famous violinist Joshua Bell to understand the context in which the perception and priorities of human beings change. On a busy weekday morning, Joshua Bell was playing the violin in the corridor of a subway station in New York. He was using a violin worth 3.5 million dollars (made in 1730). He played a few Bach pieces for about forty-five minutes. During that time, thousands of people crossed him in the station. Few people stayed for a while. About twenty gave him money but continued to walk by their normal pace. He collected $32. When he finished playing and silence took over, no one applauded, nor was there any recognition. Few days before, Joshua Bell was sold out at a theatre in Boston, and the price of an average ticket was $100.

Through this experiment, it was realised that the place, context, and priorities of the human being are extremely important to judge the value of the product or service. So was the case for the balloon containing the 'air of Paris'. Had the case been that the vendor was not selling it below the Eiffel Tower or that he was selling at any small street of Paris, he would not have gotten the value of the product he was selling. Hence, when students asked me about brand value, I fumbled for few minutes and started explaining the concept of value in different situations, the way an economist understands it.

Many years before 2007, I had a similar experience in another context. It was during the same visit in Paris. I was a casual tourist at Montmartre, a famous place for budding painters and artists to showcase their capabilities. It was a sunny Sunday morning in springtime, and the weather was excellent. Lots of music, good paintings, and the smell of good food were around me. In front of Place du Tertre, a lonely cello player was playing a beautiful tune of his own creation. Many people were around him, applauding and requesting for other tunes (Mozart, Bach, and Bellini). I bought a cassette from him. Long before Internet days, it was not possible for me to go back and track whether that cello player became popular. Today, when I find Jean-Pierre Lignian has downloadable MP3 music, an iTunes account in his name, I go back and check the cassette in my old dusty music player and then rediscover the value of the product in a different way. The cassette has brought a new meaning as I know and understand that this has become an antique product. And now, its value is much more than the few francs hat I spent to buy the music. More importantly, the setting of Montmartre on that morning was electrifying, and people wanted to have a wonderful experience which itself created the perception and priorities for developing the value of the music and paintings. Jean-Pierre Lignian was the greatest catalyst in developing that eternal moment.

The perception is very important by which the value is being created, and the seller must understand whether the buyer can be communicated through the promotional channel so that both sides attach similar value to the product or service. In a different way, economists have defined 'consumer and producer's surplus' to describe how much value stakeholders are deriving.

I visited many other places around Paris, and a few things pushed me to think whether values (tangible and intangible) are divisible. One of such things is an invitation for dinner at the second-floor restaurant on the Eiffel Tower. We heard about French cuisine and delicacies. However, having a dinner on the Eiffel Tower has a separate brand value which is much more than the food we experienced. Perhaps, it is the overall experience, not the food only, that produces a value. So products and related services together offer a value which is of many times more than the individual value (such as food at any good French restaurant and tariff to climb up the Eiffel Tower).

When I check my old album, Champs-Elysées, the famous avenue, produces nostalgic yet similar feelings in my mind. The road is full of popular shops, restaurants, nightclubs, cabarets (such as, Lido). The very interesting thing which struck me was the display of sculptures as a live exhibition on the pavement of Champs-Elysées. Artists and sculptors must be dying to have a single presence on the boulevard of Champs-Elysées as this is a proper communication to increase their brand value by many folds. Professors in marketing classes explain the brand with delicate definitions and concepts with lots of tools for measuring the brand equity. However, the subjective element behind the value (or economic value) of a brand cannot be ignored. It is the seller's perception which tries to establish the value in the buyer's mind. But there is no linear connectivity between seller's perception and how the client will look into the product and define the value. Communication makes a big change, and it informs a buyer how she/he should define the brand value of the product and service.

Now, let us have an idea of how a new product can create a brand through its overwhelming presence and communication skill by the creator. Impressionism is the nineteenth century art movement which was originated with a group of Paris-based artists and whose independent exhibitions brought them to the limelight during the 1870s and 1880s. These painters were ready to break away from creating only realistic pieces and wanted to start capturing what a camera could not—the colourful details of the image. This group of experimental French painters led a revolt against the established art salons and created playful and artistic paintings to evoke the energy of the image without replicating the actual picture. They received harsh criticism from the art community and were not allowed to display their paintings in museums. Later on, the critics tried to find out a trend in their painting and followed the name impressionism from the title of a work by Claude Monet, *Impression Soleil Levant* (impression, sunrise). The discovery of the camera and increasing influence of photography was a challenge to modern painting in the late nineteenth century. Impressionism provided a fresh interest in the paintings, giving a new dimension, not only in technicalities but also from an aesthetic sense. Characteristics of an impressionist painting include gross brush strokes, a new dimension of light and shade with different colours, and a subtle sense of 3D. As a result, common ordinary subjects become uncommon with the sense of movement as a crucial element of human perception and experience from different angles. Impressionism as a concept provides us learning on how with the distinct yet strict product quality you can create a new brand. There are many such examples all over the world by which a new product becomes a hit when it comes up instantaneously and then turn into a successful brand. Everyone knows the success of Apple. So product is in the heart of the brand

4

in this case, and communication of the product quality is extremely strong in the mind of the client.

Through another example, I would like to depict a case where perception of the same product also changes over time. When I travelled to Tanzania for the first time, I was struck by a beautiful billboard of Masai holding a cell phone, clearly communicating *empowerment* with the newly introduced phone in the market. The cheerful Masai in the advertisement was standing in the middle of an African jungle, portraying that he was the 'king of Serengeti'. It was a strong message expressed through that billboard that the phone can make you empowered and, even inside the forest, you would feel yourself strong enough in terms of your connectivity with the rest of the world. The billboard was on the Bagamoyo Road, Dar es Salaam. The scenic beauty of the road is praiseworthy. On the right side you find the glimpse of blue Indian Ocean; the road goes up and down with a few baobab trees around, and several European style houses make the whole scene picturesque.

Ten years later, when I drove by the same road, many things got changed. There are now high-rise buildings, but in general, the beauty of the road remains. What is interesting is that there are many billboards that have come up but the same one was still depicting an advertisement of a cell phone, most astonishingly by Airtel now. The picture in the billboard has now changed, and it communicates that you are connected anywhere with anyone even when you are stranded in the middle of a traffic jam. The billboard with the Masai is now replaced with a photo of a huge traffic jam and some words are written in Kiswahili. Hence, the communication changed from empowerment to the mere speed of connectivity. So is the perception of the people who are getting influenced by the cell phone advertisement changed too? So what is the brand value? Is it constant? Is it the same throughout the world? Is it the same for all people? Answers are all conditional and depend on a large number of socio-economic factors. Hence, even for a marketing question of what is brand, we convert the question to what is the value of a product or service measured from various perspectives.

Many a time, we find generic development of brand in a more macro set-up. For example, these days most of the emerging countries are trying to attract tourist's attention, foreign investment, etc. through a worldwide campaign. 'Incredible India', 'Malaysia: Truly Asia', etc. are rated as very important propaganda in this part of the world. Imagine a consumer who believes in these advertisements and develops a notion about the country and then tries to convert his/her belief into experience. Here, an expectation must match with the reality. Hence, the generic brand value has a dangerous side and that specific experience may not match with expectation or the brand value created by the advertisement. The ever-increasing crowd in Indian tourist spots pushes companies to develop segmented tourism market for different groups of the people. So when a foreigner would like to stay in a luxury hotel and to have a special entry to tourist spots, his or her experience will not match with the experience of backpackers. Also, competition among countries may force each country to develop imaginary offerings or new products such as experiencing a 'crowded traditional bazaar'. Competition can improve the brand image in terms of new experience, but it can also cause damage when expectation and actual experience does not match. Through social media, macro brand image of a country is also being built where people write and share their travelogues. Many a time, Internet provides a negative image, and it remains on the top of the mind unless the experience differs. There are many countries that provide wonderful opportunities to do business, but a potential negative image can ruin this. With the behest of the United Nations, I took up an assignment on trade liberalisation issues of Papua New Guinea (PNG). I also travelled there a couple of times. While doing the study, I was amazed by the strong economic fundamentals of PNG and developed my own idea about the country before visiting Port Moresby. PNG has a strong base on minerals, including gold and copper; it also has crude oil and natural gas. It is geographically well located, not far from Australia. During the first half of 2000 it has progressed substantially, experiencing current account surplus, reduced inflation, higher growth, etc. However, reports and news published in the Internet provided a negative feeling in terms of security, and I am sure it could have significant impact on the foreign investment and development process. Some Internet reports also highlighted that the country had high risk for investment and also showed concern about safety. With great doubt, I boarded the Air New Guinea flight from Singapore for an overnight journey to Port Moresby. It reached Jacksons International Airport early in the morning. The small sleepy airport just woke up. It was foggy outside. Hotel's driver introduced himself, and I boarded the van. I had many such eerie feelings in Africa, and I was deliberately ignoring them. The van was running through a beautiful road (not very wide) with classic country music in the radio. To ease the feeling, I started speaking to the driver without divulging that I was a first timer. The cheerful aboriginal driver started talking about his family, about the city, and more importantly, how the country has been now exposed globally. At the hotel, I was surprised by the level of security. It took almost ten minutes to cross the layers of security cordon. At the reception, I suddenly discovered that I was cordoned by army personnel. After few moments of shock, I realised that they were from the US and perhaps living in the same hotel. Inside the room also, there was detailed security instruction. I joined the breakfast table with other officers from the United Nations and started discussing about the security system. During the day, we went out in a much-secured vehicle and met government officials. Everywhere we have been given a picture of risk and security. We also experienced the similar thing in the bank. Marry, a Commerce Ministry official, was helping us to understand the economic as well as business environment. She was escorting us to officers, and in between I was trying to get the answer of my mystery question about real security threat in a common man's day-to-day life. I noted the presence of a few journalists from Australia while I was presenting the summary of the study, and some of them were arguing in favour of cautious opening of the PNG economy. During my stay, I went to the school where Marry's daughters study, also to the neighbourhood she lived, and to the common market and did not find the pulse of insecurity in local life. The life in Port Moresby was very normal, but as I saw in Australia, markets closed down as the sun set in. This is nothing unusual in that part of the world. Some uncertainty at the political level and conflict among some powerful groups are not uncommon in this world, but this heightened security concern seemed to be a bit artificial. The question baffled me continuously about the negative country image and the difference between specific and general views about this heightened security concern. Indeed it became a good market for security products and services. This could have helped some investors also to derive a benefit due to lack of competition in the market. Since then, I have been trying to correlate whether the negative image of PNG is related towards rent-seeking behaviour in the economy. When I was coming back, in the airport, I wanted to change my local currency but found that the sole bank in the airport was closed. I was told by the security officer that the bank would open when the flight from Brisbane came at 10.30. What was the relation between these two? The security officer informed me that all the money exchanged by this bank would come from Brisbane only. They don't keep anything here—the security concern. Poor me again started thinking about the transaction cost versus the benefit of heightened security concern and waited till the bank opened.

2

Beyond Economic Fundamentals: Something Else Also Matters

Spectacular growth of emerging economies in 1990s and debacle of developed economies in the twenty-first century have raised renewed interest towards the development model of underdeveloped economies. Though the literature is full of fascinating development models which are widely being taught in our part of the world, the new interests mostly look into holistic models of development and sometimes go beyond the traditional literature of economics. Multilateral agencies also contributed significantly in enriching this literature. Issues such as establishing the linkage between trade and poverty, inclusive growth driven by the Millennium Development Goals (MDG), bridging the digital divide as a tool for development, role of traditional knowledge, reliable institutions, governance, etc. in shaping the development process have become very prominent. With the proliferation of this literature, experts from other subject areas are also equally active in bringing out new models for development. Socio-economic, cultural, and historical factors play significant roles in this. Professor Amartya Sen argued that 'critical openings as a cultural factor and a positive view towards Heterogeneity'[1] act as catalysts in collecting debate and discussion, and as a result, open society is able to nurture different types of development models. Hence, society's basic tenets, its cultural root, also play important roles in determining the path for development. Many economies have unexplored or yet-to-be highlighted critical factors which interestingly play important roles, and we tend to ignore them as they are very subtle and don't have a proper yardstick to measure.

I was stranded at Port Moresby airport with my Chinese and Korean friends. To kill time of eight hours in the small airport lounge, we started sharing development experiences of India, China, and Korea. Several common issues were discussed and then came up the issue of family values and the responsibility towards parents and children. All of us agreed that in our countries, we as parents remain very vigilant about the academic/intellectual progress of our children even when they are at the age of a toddler. This is quite unique in our societies which boosts our aspiration from the childhood towards knowledge gain and thereby contributes in overall human capital development independent of the effort from the state. The literature on human capital, including the endogenous growth models, duly considers these factors to analyse growth and development. There are middle-income countries in the world which, due to the lack of family focus on education, suffer in creating the pool of skilled workers. Hence, the stability of our economies comes from the strong base not only in manufacturing and services sector and of cheap labour but also from the pool of skilled workers due to a strong base in education.

In developing this early education system, Indian grandparents, many a time, take care as well as support the early education of their grandchildren, especially for urban working couples. This unique balance, though eroding out, still has significant contributions in our development process. I have noticed the close interaction of grandparents with the teachers in my son's school which reiterated the thought how family bonding is important in nurturing India's most precious economic variable: skilled labour force. In Delhi, I had the experience of teaching mathematics to a few Korean children in early 1990s and found quite similar seriousness among mothers. During the discussion, our Chinese friend also highlighted that state education system can only play a complementary role, but it all depends on how parents and family members take care of the children at home and state has limited control on this. This family value manifests the Asian tradition and its social system which is almost missing in many of the developed economies. After spending hours of such discussion with gallons of beers, sandwiches, and many silent moments in the middle of a brilliant picturesque sunset over the mountain, our Chinese friend suddenly asked me, 'Is it true that large number of Indian men and women take care of their aging parents and they stay together?' I nodded my head. 'Perhaps the role of grandparents as economic agents in India's development requires rigorous research,' he murmured.

Many other countries have unique features which are not purely economic but have similar contribution in the new growth model. Experts collect these so-called best practices and develop their possible replication in other parts of the world. However, many such issues are unique, imbibed in the progress of civilisation dating back to thousands of years. They can't be copied and implemented in other places overnight. As an example, we can mention the cleanliness as fetish for the people from Thailand. We are all aware of growth histories of 'Asian tigers' through 'flying geese' model in which Japanese MNEs invest and ignite SME growth through diffusion of technology. Hardly have we looked into the social progress. Along with the manufacturing growth, the Kingdom of Thailand slowly became a major tourist destination in the South East Asian countries. I noted that most of the Thai families love to spend weekends not at home, rather in some other place such as at nearby islands or beaches. Hence, tourism as a market originally had an internal demand push. Over the years, along with the higher growth, tourism models also got matured. Thai government's continuous attention towards service quality and promotion of competition is praiseworthy. Very interestingly, the obsession towards cleanliness ensured that budget hotels maintain certain standards of hygiene. Soon through the proliferation of numerous hotels across Thailand, boarding cost came down. Today, budget hotels, small motels, and resorts provide highly clean rooms including toilets without any luxury but at very cheap price which you can imagine to get only in Star Hotels in India. Even, the toilets in shopping malls of Bangkok are places to visit. Most people love to wear clean white shirts, and the section of personal care in any department store always has an amazing mix of local and foreign collections. The famous or infamous sex tourism of Thailand survives on the simple idea: high level hygiene and low HIV growth. In fact, since 1991, yearly new infections have fallen dramatically. Thailand is one of the very first countries to have achieved the sixth Millennium Development Goal, to begin to reverse the spread of HIV/AIDS by 2015, well in advance of the target date. This success of Thailand must first and foremost be attributed to courageous and visionary top-level leadership displayed at a relatively early stage of the epidemic. The success lies in the process of communication from the public health agencies, government ministries, the military, non-governmental organizations, and the media. This was possible because of society's engagement in open dialogue and obsession of basic protection as part of their inclination towards hygiene and safe sex. People around the world visit Thailand and enjoy their holidays, but when they go back, they carry two things in their memory: one is cleanliness; second is the kind of greetings they received in the country, forgetting all others.

When I first landed at the Julius Nyerere International Airport, Dar es Salaam, I mentally mapped the country like any other LDC in Asia with rampant poverty, weak institutions, rent-seeking activities, and slow macroeconomic progress. At the beginning of the century, Tanzania's GDP growth was around 4–4.5 per cent. The city was buzzing with economic activities and the significant presence of Indians both in business and profession. I used to get glimpses of the city while going to the Institute of Finance Management from our guest house at Namanga. We were staying in a sleepy neighbourhood, and the new US embassy building was coming up just next to us. The memory of attacks on the US embassy in Dar was still fresh. My old friend Sandip was working in the same city, and fortunately I got his company in the leisure time. I still remember that one day after a spell of rain when Sandip was driving his big vehicle cautiously on the undulating road, one person wearing an army uniform suddenly jumped in front of the car. We stopped and rolled down the window glass. 'You have hit me, Muhindi [Indian],' he shouted and said that he would put us in jail as he was going to call the police. I was extremely scared. Sandip was cool and said, 'Hakuna matata, I can manage.' He got down from the car. I was sweating inside. 'Jambo,' he said, and then I realized he was going to negotiate, and finally a deal was met with $20. I have come across almost similar incidents in my follow-up visits which might sometimes start from the airport itself. Sandip's housemaid knew that my favourite dish was ugali with Mchuzi wa samaki (cornmeal mush with fish curry), and I was amazed every time by her care in preparing the food and serving so nicely. With broken English, she used to express her gratitude. I got to know about the struggles these ladies had to do because of the burden of the big family they had and managing of high medical expenditure due to all-round malnutrition and invasion of malaria. Despite so much misery, they were working with patience and sincerity. I observed the same spirit as I noticed in Bangkok among Thai and Phillipino girls working as housemaids. At IFM, many faculties were educated in the British system, and we had much debate about suitable growth models, independent monetary policy, and modes of liberalisation. The sense of determination among them was high to enhance the economic growth rate, but they were equally concerned about corruption leading to low FDI and investment in general. Everybody was vocal about the image of the country and wanted to change it. They felt that Tanzania had potentiality to grow. Some level of corruption is quite common in a developing world. Rather than the ground-level corruption, the country's overall image is more important for attracting investment.

Ten years after, it was past midnight in Dar. I did not keep track of time while in typical *adda* (gossips in a group) with Sushen (my student) at his place. I was hesitating and feeling a bit unnerved thinking about how to go back to the hotel. Sushen was insisting to drop me by his car, and I did not want that. Finally, he called a taxi. Dar had recently introduced city taxi. It arrived within five minutes. 'Karibu, Rafiki, habari [Welcome, my friend, how are you]? Twelve thousand shilling and I'll drop you safely.' My heart was beating fast. I waved my hand to Sushen, and the taxi picked up the speed. I started talking to the driver and somehow engaged him in the discussion, carefully noticing whether he was taking any unknown road. When the taxi reached close to the hotel, I discovered the shortage of change in my wallet. Reaching the hotel, I told the driver, 'Please wait. I'll ask the reception to give me change.' 'Hey, Rafiki, wait!' said the driver. 'Give me Ts8,000 only and I sacrifice Ts4,000. You are my guest, I enjoyed talking to you. We know India can help us in growing fast. Above all, Gandhi is our inspiration.' For a few seconds, I was awestruck. 'Asante Sana' (thank you very much), I saluted. Inside, my hotel room phone was ringing loudly. Sushen was enquiring whether I reached safely. I was thinking of the sticker 'Atithi Devo Bhava' (Gusts are god) pasted on the Delhi taxi and the perennial harassment with our 'Kali-pili' (black and yellow taxi).

Today, Tanzania is one of the fastest growing African economies. Key drivers of growth in the short and medium term include private consumption, exports and gross fixed capital, tourism revenues, foreign investment, and aid. Substantial reform, large investments by foreign firms, and government's effort to diffuse the growth has pushed the economy one notch above permanently. The growth rate will be around 7.5 per cent or above expectedly in next few years. Many Indian corporate giants are now present, and many others are on the verge of entering to tap the growing middle-class market.

The world has witnessed high growth in the midst of corruption, and in contrast, sometimes honest rulers failed to control corruption which affected the growth badly. In the case of Tanzania, it caught into classic principal–agent problem as narrated by Alan Beattie in his book *False Economy*. He argued that though President Nyerere himself was an inspiring and iconic figure, he did not have full control on bureaucracy and other major stakeholders who indulged into corruption. Comparing this with the Philippines, Alan put forward his points that corruption created a barrier for competition and allowed monopoly return to few. The Philippines also opened up the economy strategically to attract foreign investment (such as free capital flow) which induced more money to come in. This in turn helped the ruler to flourish further. The nexus between investors and political bosses helped the crony capitalism to thrive in the Philippines. Hence, corruption was systematic and organised based on a network of information. In contrast, corruption in Tanzania was mostly due to information gap, various divides in the economy, and a general phenomenon of rent-seeking behaviour. With the effort of some leaders through setting up few good institutions, information gap has been brought down; investment climate has also been improved. Contribution of aid agency is equally praiseworthy in bringing back the image of the country. UNCTAD in 2011 also recognised the progress of Tanzania. As the corruption was not deeply organised, along with the economic reform, the nation turned around fast, its image got changed, and it is recognised as the eighth most favourite destination for doing business [2] among low-income countries.

Since the beginning of 2011, we have started discussing intensely the emerging crisis in Europe and then more specifically about Greece. Soon, other countries such as Italy and Portugal have joined the league. Low productivity, high sovereign debt, unmanageable government expenditure, and above all, lack of independent monetary policy (euro being an international currency) have played havoc. Debate is still unsettled about the possible future course in terms of dynamic policy options for these countries.

Italy, being one of the major industrialized countries, derives its GDP mostly from services (73 per cent) and industry (25 per cent). Agriculture contributes only 2 per cent as per 2010 statistics. Its long-term growth history shows that growth has been decelerating almost steadily in last thirty years, and it declined steadily since 2008.

Figure 1: Italy's Real GDP Percentage Change (Five-Year Moving Average)

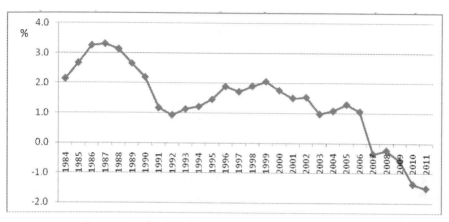

Source: Calculated by author from the EIU data.

Very interestingly, Italy's northern part has a well-developed industrial base, and its southern region is dominated by agricultural production. The Italian economy is driven in large part by the manufacture of high-quality consumer goods produced by small and medium-sized enterprises, many of them family-owned. Tourism, machinery, iron and steel, chemicals, food processing, textiles, motor vehicles, clothing, footwear, ceramics, and agricultural goods are the major sectors of the economy. It generates wealth through value addition in industrial design (such as in parts and components, furniture, ceramics, and metal products) and aligning fashion and style with textile/apparel. Design and fashion are the core catalyst in enhancing growth in most of the economic activities including services (such as in tourism). The energy of growth has been coming from the 4Fs: food and wine, fashion, furniture and products of home décor and building materials, and fabricated metal products including auto components. In 2006 the 4Fs generated an added value of about 142 billion euros, or about 65 per cent of Italy's overall manufacturing value added at factor cost (219 billion euros). The 4Fs employ around 3.3 million people.[3]

Table 1: The value added of the '4Fs' of 'Made in Italy': some international comparisons

The '4Fs' of 'Made in Italy' manufacturing	Value added at factor cost (billion euro) Year 2006	International comparisons	Value added at factor cost (billion euro), Year 2006
Italy—food and wine	19	France and Spain—manufacture of motor vehicles	16
Italy—fashion and luxury	26	France, Germany, and UK—manufacture of aircraft and spacecraft	24
Italy—furniture and building materials	16	Finland, Sweden, and UK—manufacture of radio, television, and communications apartments	15
Italy—fabricated metal products, machinery, plastic, and rubber products	81	UE-27 (including Italy)—manufacture of pharmaceuticals, medicinal chemicals, and botanic products	71

Source: Marco Fortis (2010).[4]

I have been invited by Prof. Fabio Sdogati and his Greek wife for a dinner while I was in Milan in 2011. As a typical middle-class Indian, I was tensed in the afternoon whether I was having the right kind of dress to go to the dinner and that too in Milan. During the day, I had the opportunity to have a quick glimpse of Via Montenapoleone, undoubtedly the world's (one of the) best fashion streets. While walking on the portico, with a little more careful eye, you can notice how each person is conscious about the style, brand, and beauty; it goes with age, gender and income level. The elegance and confidence of people around was noteworthy.

Fifty years back, Milan was not a major landmark in the fashion industry. It was far behind of Paris, New York, and London. Very few Italian designers were having international reputation. However, the respect towards art and culture has been engraved in the society for centuries, and people used to appreciate the skill of local dressmakers. Gentlemen ordered suits from traditional bespoke tailors, while their wives and daughters patronised whichever local dressmaker exhibited the greatest skill in replicating the latest fashion from Paris. A skill was hidden inside the four walls, as traditional and modest housewives used to stitch their own clothes, hunting the best fabric from the markets and copying the latest style. Over the years, this skilled yet cheaper labour fuelled the growth of the Italian fashion industry. Marshall Plan after the Second World War provided great opportunity to skilled artisans, uprooted from the hill towns of the north and the poor villages of the south in search of a livelihood. Along with this, the investment made on machinery created an unrivalled garment manufacturing capability. Coupled with this was the historic coincidence of the emergence of new generation native design talents who wanted to have a distinctive identity. The entire effort took the advantage of global fascination towards 'Made in Italy' and the inner strength of marketing. Talented new designers showed impressive balance between commercial aspect and quality based on brand value. The three Fontana sisters, Zoe, Giovanna, and Micol, were typical of those emerging talents who grasped the new possibilities in later 1940s. In the following decades, Italian designers got reputation through Hollywood movies as many considered the distinctiveness in the form of chic, understated and realistic in contrast to French designs which are sophisticated and also quite elaborate. The linear, practical, and user-friendly design revolution also positively influenced Italian industrial sectors (in furniture, home décor, ceramics, components, and metal products). Some designers like Versace, Giorgio Armani, and Laura Biagiotti became industrialists eventually and pushed the sector as one of Italy's major money spinners.

I was walking with Fabio through Via Andrea Doria towards Milan Central Station (a piece of stunning architecture). It was dusk; beautiful buildings, roundabouts, and boulevards were becoming majestic with evening lights. I was explaining my surprise about the detailed marble work in Duomo (Milan Cathedral) and the shopping arcade (Galleria Vittorio Emanuele II) with the presence of the latest range of products offered by Louis Vuitton and Prada. I also informed him that a recent Bengali movie was filmed there; hence, he might see many Bengali tourists in the coming days. Soon we reached the restaurant (l'Osteria del Treno) and were received by his wife. The restaurant opens at 8 p.m. sharp, and you need to book tables beforehand. This is one of the pioneering restaurants in the 'slow food' movement in Italy. Slow food as opposed to the 'fast food' is the new trend which has swept the entire continent in recent times. Like any other food-loving Italian, Fabio was busy in explaining the food in details including its minute details (such as from which part of Italy the spices are coming or how the meat has been marinated, etc.). With course after course when we finished, the clock was about to strike eleven, but we were not feeling heavy (beauty of slow dining). During the entire duration, I heard Fabio's vocal criticism and appreciation about the current policy regime. However, my interest was on direct and indirect contribution of fashion and design industry on Italy's economy and its sustainability. In early 1990s the trade surplus in textile and apparel industry was almost equivalent to deficit in food and energy sources like oil. Recent studies also show that Italy has permanently shifted to higher value-added goods, and exports did not get the hit even when euro was appreciated (advantage of low elasticity). But under the current situation when the developed world is slowing down, Italy's biggest challenge is to reach newly emerging economies which will be the future source of revenue. For that, companies need to develop economies of scale and different pricing strategy. The greatest dilemma is whether lower prices will dilute the brand value. Fabio informed me that Italian companies are choosing countries like Tunisia, Albania, etc. for outsourcing their production. The industry is also receiving government incentives. Italy's biggest trade partners are European countries such as Germany, France, UK, etc. but the new markets are somewhere else where Asian countries are highly active in which 'low price and high quality' set the mood of competition. Does it mean that Italian companies will go for mass production or face the peculiar competition such as selling 500 shirts by Vietnamese/Bangladeshi companies worth of $2 each versus one piece of $1,000 Armani suit?

Italy's fashion industry grew without much creative opposition. In the continuing absence of significant new brands, the biggest fashion news from Italy in 1980s and 1990s has been the successful regeneration of old luxury goods houses such as Prada and Gucci and manufacturing innovation fuelled by groups such as Gruppo Finanziario Tessile (GFT)—the mere uniform supplier turned into powerhouse of luxury fashion, manufacturing for Armani, Valentino, and Ungaro. However, the new driver is the youth fantasy. Traditional Italian brands need to develop more futuristic products satisfying tomorrow's youth who want more than 'understated elegance' and more than what is 'real'. Hence, Italian brands now need to compete with themselves in terms of innovation, and at the same time, they also require to focus on economies of scale for their penetration in South Africa, Brazil, India, UAE, etc.

While strolling back to the hotel, I saw a huge pile of garbage bags (almost two storied high) on the street corner. I expressed my surprise. 'The city is being cleaned and so much of garbage is in one place!' Fabio said, 'These bags will go to Germany, and they are waiting to get lifted. We export garbage to Germany and import energy [made out of this].' 'Why do you need to export? You have the technology.' With a smile he answered that there was no design and fashion component in this sector, and so Italy is seriously uncompetitive.

By the way, now there are few MNCs who have established their plants to generate energy from waste disposal in Italy.

3

Food and Culture in Global Context

Every country is different not only because of its economic structure but also due to its cultural identity. We have never been able to agree on a definition of culture, but in general, it includes knowledge, principle, custom, laws, etc. Cross-cultural difference is very important in defining the identity of a country and an individual in the global context. Social scientists J. Zvi Namenwirth and Robert Philip Weber argue that culture is a system of ideas which constitute the design for living based on values and some unwritten social rules and guidance. Food is definitely providing a dimension in understanding the identity of a society and individual. Though in global context cuisine of different countries have gotten influenced with the cross-border movement of people around the world, there still exist distinct identities. So Chinatown or Little India is not a strange place in big cities where Indian and Chinese food and culture thrive amidst of the dominant position of the host country. There are many writings on food and culture as binding force in today's globalisation. In 2002, the Council of Europe constituted a working group (Working Group on Food) to explore how food affects the individual in the context of diverse culture and promote tolerance. In a unique experiment, faculty from Tel Aviv University, University College Dublin, University of Toulouse, etc. tried to understand whether food can act as ambassador in bringing two cultures together and make an attempt to solve the conflicts. The discussion has been summarised in the book *Culinary Cultures of Europe:*

Identity, Diversity and Dialogues co-edited by Darra Goldstein and Kathrin Merkle in 2005, where authors focused on food as a driver for social process, not as commodity. According to Goldstein, food is emotionally linked to an individual. If we are able to channel those emotions into something positive, it's really wonderful, but all too often they are diverted into something negative. All over the world, food from other places are adopted and evolved with local tastes. Whether it is California roll (sushi converted to American tastes) or biriyani (whose tastes differ widely in Lucknow, Hyderabad, or Kolkata), nobody takes it offensively as it is not hurting that seriously to Japanese culture or that to authentic Mughlai cuisine. However, Goldstein and other researchers made an attempt to bring Israelis and Palestinians to the same dinner table, but they utterly failed and understood that deep-rooted mistrust was the main cause. People have a feeling that food in other countries has not been adopted, rather they are appropriated (stolen) and then the issue becomes serious. Authors gave examples of falafel (fava beans or chickpeas mashed with spices and then fried. It is generally used to stuff pita sandwiches). This Arab food is popular in every family (Jews, Arabs, or any other) and in the entire Middle East. However, Israelis have made it commercially successful in many parts of the world especially in Europe. Falafel has become an icon of Israeli cuisine. Goldstein and Merkle argued that many Palestinians felt that this was another thing taken away from them. Hence, food has become all the more an important political issue between Palestine and Israel. In other countries, chefs are having a number of TV shows, writing books focusing on good health, culinary adventures, etc. but chefs in Israel and Palestine are focusing on political goodwill (such as Erez Komrovsky and Mahmoud Sfadi cooking together and making public statements too). Chefs becoming political ambassadors and making attempts to bring harmony among community is unheard of.

So adoption and assimilation of food can help people to come together. This has pushed me to think about bringing Indian and Pakistani cuisine together and promoting them. The food from North India and Pakistan are close to each other, but it is the time to explore the uniqueness. Big cities like Delhi and Mumbai can invite Pakistani chefs in speciality restaurants. This will not only bring food together but along with this music, literature, and culture can be shared. This will bridge the gap which has been there over the decades. We are so close, yet so far. More people-to-people contact at the grass-roots level can definitely increase our collective wisdom. As international business between the countries are getting regularised (Pakistan's granting MFN status to India), these restaurants will thrive with the business meetings in coming days. It might start with mere culinary adventure by normal citizens, but the visit can be made more cherished one through a dose of information sharing. However, the flip side will be the security fear and possibility of backlash. Government is required to be bold enough in taking care of these issues considering the deemed benefit.

Food can provide such a wonderful bridge between cultures. In one of such incidents, which reminds me how the universal brotherhood is reflected just by the way food is served, we went to an Ethiopian restaurant where food was served in a same plate for four of us who were dining over a semi-official meeting. It was a surprise to me that a big plate was kept in the middle of the table. The plate was covered by big size bread and different food items were kept on the bread in different corners. The flat bread injera (a large sourdough about twenty inches in diameter, made from fermented flour) is part of the common system of Ethiopian dining. We ordered for some shiro wot with the spinach and cottage cheese dish, chicken firfir/doro alicha, etc. When we were tearing the bread and using our hands to eat, the meeting suddenly became quite informal and an 'all equal' concept prevailed. All four of us, citizens of different countries, without looking into our individual identity, had the food leisurely and got involved in the discussion. Meeting was fruitful and it developed a sense of satisfaction and food was the main catalyst.

Boo Sung, invited a few of us for a dinner. He mentioned that it was informal, and authentic home-made Korean food would be served. It was December 2010, Seoul's evening temperature was hovering around –7 to –10 degrees Celsius. Our team consisted of American, French, Indian, Sri Lankan, and a few Koreans. We walked through the beautiful Insadong market (a kind of heritage street having shops of apparels, handicrafts, and ethnic goods). We reached a small house having a courtyard in the middle. An old lady welcomed us. She opened one of the rooms. A typical Korean house with wooden floor and was already warmed up as Boo Sung made a prior reservation. As far as I remember, the name of the restaurant was Koong. A speciality in serving traditional homestyle food with its uniqueness, this restaurant stands out as its Kaesong dumplings (flour pouches stuffed mostly with pork, tofu, and chives) perhaps have the thinnest flour skin. When all of us were rubbing our hands to warm ourselves, three sets of kimchi salads were served made from cabbages, radish, etc. along with dumplings. All of us jumped over the food like small kids. Soups (guk) are served generally with the main dish. A number of side dishes (banchan) were brought one after another (as in Bengali culture). Some of them were grilled and some steamed. A series of sweets and Korean tea at the end are also worth mentioning. During this long dinner, sitting on the floor, all of us started sharing our own dining culture. The similarity and dissimilarity, etiquette, dining style, etc. were put up sometimes seriously and sometimes with humour. A friendly dinner became a rich source of knowledge for everybody. Boo Sung started narrating the preparation style of some items and their uniqueness. Food always plays a binding role among humans even though they are from different cultures. It stimulates discussion, provides opportunity for networking, and could be a source of satisfaction.

If you don't enjoy a dinner, it could have an opposite effect and sometimes could be even disastrous. It was in 2003 at Bangkok when Arjun Sengupta and Bibek Debroy came to ESCAP for a conference and I took them to a dinner. During the day, Mr Lam instigated them, saying, good foods are always cheap and one must experience local food in a local set up. In the evening, we walked to a Thai restaurant. The ambience was quite nice, Thai music was being played by a couple, with good artwork all over. We, all foodies, closely looked into the menu card. I remained cautious as even English versions did not provide much information, but Debroy wanted to go for an experiment. My knowledge was limited to *khao phat kai* (chicken fried rice), *phat si-io* (stir-fried noodles), *tom yam* (hot and sour soup), and some curries. As a desert, my all-time favourite was *khao niao mamuang* (sticky rice cooked with milk and served with ripe mango). But finally, going beyond simplicity, we ordered for exotic food which included wild boar. I am allergic to seafood including prawn, and with great difficulty I explained to the waiter not to give *kung* (prawn). Exotic smell of the food was all around. When the smoky food was served, we could not believe that we ordered so much. With awesome taste, all of us were enjoying the meal. Suddenly, I started feeling uncomfortable. There was a sense of itching all over my body, and my voice was getting choked. I must have eaten something for which my body started reacting. The sauces given on the food must have seafood content, and then I discovered crabmeat (*boo* or *pu*). My lips swelled, and I was unable to speak. My two guests were enjoying the meal, and I was thinking how to get out of this, reach home quickly, and take some medicine.

We were in the middle of the discussion about Indian politics, decision-making process, bureaucracy, etc. I started having a stomach ache. After finishing the dinner, I insisted for the taxi, but Arjun Sengupta wanted to walk. 'Hotel is just ten minutes away.' But I had to take the taxi anyway as my apartment was not nearby and I forced. After reaching home, I took some medicine with the hope that it would subside. The food also triggered stomach infection. My situation was like what Kaushik Basu described about himself after having the dinner during the Japanese Economic Association Conference.[5] The only exception was that I knew few Thai words and could give a call to a doctor and in an extreme case could ask for a taxi to the hospital. Later on, I had many experiences in Thailand about exotic food, and I was always mentally prepared and carried medicine. My boss gave a farewell dinner to one of our colleagues at ESCAP. I was enjoying the soup till the time somebody told me it was crocodile soup. Thankfully, my body was immune to Thai food by then. My living in Thailand was of great influence on me. I used to go to local Chinese vegetable markets, buying them with all my funny expressions. Gradually, some sellers used to make attempts to explain to me with indications which vegetables to cook with what meat and what spices and sauce. I also made attempts to cook them (obviously most of the time it was thrown to the dustbin due to their unbearable taste made out of my innovation). But I enjoyed through and through. After all, cooking is the best stress buster.

Food reflects different kinds of identities. Individual identity reflects from the personal choice whereas collective identity is more complex which gets influenced by geographic differences, religious proscriptions, and ethnic priorities. Sometimes all these identities create confusion about the true collective identity. Bengalis, mostly being non-vegetarians, find their identity in conflict with majority of Hindu identity both in North and South India. It is difficult to develop boundaries based on food as it moves along with people, adapted over the years, and now get influenced by the force of globalisation. India's urban food habit is changing. Department stores are filled up with new items. Getting Chinese sauce or Italian pasta sauce is no more a difficult proposition in fast-moving Indian cities. Vegetables like zucchini, Chinese and pink cabbage, parsley, celery, or fruits such as kiwi fruits, passion and dragon fruits, etc. were earlier available only in elite markets or stores (such as in New Market of Kolkata or Modern Bazaar in Delhi), and now they are in plenty with neighbourhood markets. Indian metros are fast engulfing the global cuisine and perhaps modifying them in their own way. The history of food reflects that vegetables and fruits moved from one country to another and then gradually became part of the host country culinary habits. For example, European cuisine changed drastically in the eighteenth century with the introduction of new-world crops such as the potato, tomato, and corn. Today the popular tomato paste used for pasta (ragu) would not have been possible unless Columbians brought it to Italy.

Agricultural trade is one of the most contentious issues in the modern history of international trade. Since its inclusion in WTO in 1995, the issue has become all the more political, dividing developing and developed economies. Subsidies in the developed countries, protectionism, sanitary, and phytosanitary issues have made the topic more complicated. Along with this, other issues such as packaging and genetically modified (GM) products have also become important in food trade. As more and more countries are adopting packaged food, it is becoming necessary to bring up policies on standards. Now even fresh vegetables and fruits are required to have certain standards due to excessive use of pesticides in some part of the world. In this background, MNCs naturally have taken the advantage in trading commodities globally, whereas local farmers in the developing world who are mostly unaware of global issues are coping up with new standards, falling prices, and demands of big MNC traders. In most parts of the developing world, the agricultural market suffers from information asymmetry and farmers become victims of this. We might be wondering where the money is going due to global food inflation. Is it the case that food production going down is pushing the price up? Prof. Brian Wright, Department of Agricultural and Resource Economics at the University of California, Berkeley, argues that during the last three decades, the global price rose mostly when production fell, but recently, grain price volatility can be linked with the stock issue. In India due to lack of scientific stock management, we might have lots of wastages and wrong forecasting about the demand. Global commodity exchanges leading to future trading of grains may have also triggered the prices. With the emergence of global food trading companies, the food culture around the world is bound to have an effect. Our food habit will be more influenced by what we get in the supermarket or what we see through advertisements. In Europe, due to fast development of regional markets, food products are increasingly being traded. So to have a quality and authentication check, European Protected Designation of Origin was introduced in 1990s which provides regional stamps. Quality and differentiations aspects are also scrutinised under this system. The US is also increasingly looking for the source details of the product even though they are originated in the country. Generic differentiation of the commodities will be the emerging dimension in food trade even within the country. The subtle differences of prices due to difference in place of origins are also already visible in Indian markets especially in metros. As food products and cuisines are becoming borderless, attempts are visible to protect the intangibles. Food traditions are now being viewed as part of cultural heritage. This is especially true in France, which applied to UNESCO to get French culinary traditions included in its Intangible Heritage List. This request has been rejected twice, in 2006 and in 2008, as has a similar application from Mexico. UNESCO has yet to designate gastronomy as a category in its heritage list.

With the progress of world civilisation, culinary habits are also changing. Several governments are showing their concern about obesity, food-related health disorders, etc. Food movements (such as slow food, eat healthy, locavore) around the world are also highly influenced by this. Common people correlate some issues with the food of certain places such as Mediterranean related to health and good life, Indian and Chinese related to exotic and spicy, etc. But still culinary adventures keep us busy for guessing about the next restaurant. The contribution of celebrities in promoting healthy recipes and other issues are also worth mentioning. Nigella Lawson, Jamie Oliver, Mario Batali, etc. along with India's own Sanjeev Kapoor are involved in developing new generation recipes which are acceptable yet healthy.

We were at Hanoi. After a day's long lectures and discussions, we were dying for good food. I, along with Yann Duval and Mia Mikic from ESCAP and Douglas Brooks from ADB, went to an ethnic Vietnamese restaurant. We all were experimenting different types of snacks and drinks. By the time the main dish was served, all of us were already full. The situation was a bit embarrassing. Every one of us was cheering up others to have something more. Meanwhile, our discussion turned towards 'big portion' food and wastage, which is very common in US, Australia, and in some parts of Europe. Everybody showed their concern. It is a custom not to waste food in every society. All of us are trained from our childhood. However, with increase in affordability wastage of food by Indians becomes very common in Indian restaurants. We don't mind if few pieces of *rotis* or a bowl of *dal* and *sabji* go to waste. Despite the 'big portion' problem, you'll find a tremendous amount of restraint in Western restaurants not to waste food. Yann shared his childhood experience when his mother remained very strict on this issue and always advised him not to take food more than what he can eat. French household dining culture ensures that children learn the value and etiquette of eating from the early stages. Jokingly Yann said that looking into the angry eyes of his mother, he always cleaned up the plate without showing any difficulty. This is not different either in India or USA as both Doug and I claimed. However, what we observed in India along with the high growth, show of opulence forced us to forget the basic values. The new generation children get confused in the tug of war between values and affordability. Our fine-dining culture is at the evolving stage. The globalisation has just touched India's culinary attention and in coming days we expect this to be matured. Along with exotic food satisfying our taste buds, we must also remember our traditional values: वृथा, तृप्तेषु भोजनम् (Food for one, whose stomach is full is waste).

4

Governance and Institutions: Twenty-First-Century Focus

The United Nations, since 1971, has named a special category of countries as least developed countries (LDCs). These countries are structurally challenged in their development process. As per the UN criteria, they are low-income countries suffering acutely in terms of weak economic structure and low human capital. They are in need of a high degree of support, in their development efforts, from the international community. As per 2012 statistics out of forty-eight identified LDCs, thirty-three are in Africa, fourteen in Asia and the Pacific, and one in Latin America. Only three countries have so far graduated from LDC status: Botswana in December 1994, Cape Verde in December 2007, and Maldives in January 2011. There was an initial confusion whether Maldives would be able to graduate in the post 2004 tsunami period. Generally, there exists an apprehension among LDCs about the smooth transition as many of the aid components are expected to get reduced once the country is ceased to be an LDC. Countries were looking for a confidence from the world community to receive concession and aid in post-graduation period. Studies show that vulnerability of these countries doesn't get reduced once they change their status. In my own research, I wanted to argue that the criteria on which the entire concept is based on may require re-look as in post-globalisation period, some LDCs will line up for graduation. In fact, several Pacific island countries are very close to the graduation threshold values. Currently, the identification of LDCs depends on predetermined threshold values of three main criteria that identify the structural handicaps: gross national income (GNI) per capita, vulnerability index, and human assets index. Each of these indices is further based on a host of variables. It is important to note that the capacity to undergo a smooth transition may vary considerably from one graduating country to the other. This is particularly evident in the present borderline cases, which illustrate a paradox: small island LDCs that apparently demonstrate the greatest and steadiest prosperity with regard to the income and human asset criteria are among the most structurally handicapped and/or vulnerable countries. On the other hand, some manufactures-exporting countries being relatively less vulnerable progressed slowly in most of the social indicators. The post-graduation strategies, therefore, differ widely from country to country considering their level and quality of development during the time of graduation. All these countries are prepared differently for the loss of concessionary treatment in the context of graduation. This is high time to bring some other issues to understand the performance of these LDCs: macroeconomic management and institutions.[6] Island LDCs are very much vulnerable to natural disasters (though many of them have relatively high per capita income and human capacity), and they are dependant significantly on external financing. In this context, serious attention is needed in efficient management of the resources availed to improve their utilisation. Refinement of macroeconomic institutions to handle the use of debt and aid is also important. In contrast to this, South Asian LDCs require more focus in managing population, health, and education. They need to give attention in upgrading the production process to achieve efficiency in their exports. Institutions leading to higher skill, better management of resources, less corruption are important to understand the stability of their status. South East Asian LDCs are more vulnerable to macroeconomic shock, hence require comprehensive management of fiscal and monetary variables along with exchange rates. These LDCs must utilize all the preferences given to them to the fullest extent. African LDCs need more focus on resource management and development of modern institutions to handle macroeconomic issues. In 2011, following the Istanbul Programme of Action (IPoA), the United Nations decided to focus on good governance (along with national ownership and leadership) to strengthen the LDCs in improving the three graduating criteria. This is expectedly going to help LDCs to graduate. IPoA chalked out a detailed plan for the decade 2011–2020.

Some time back, I was in Tanzania, and two days before returning to India, I wanted to convert my residual Tanzanian shilling to US dollar. Taking advice from one of my students, I went to a bank, requested for the conversion. The lady officer in the counter replied to me that the bank did not have sufficient foreign exchange reserve and would be obliged to serve me next time (maybe after a few days). While returning, I went to some shops (Bureau De Change) on Samora Avenue; I received the same reply. Next day I went to different banks, and everywhere the response was the same. Then, I became little paranoid and tried to understand why it was so. Later on, I asked several people (some of them are experts in finance) and received different answers. Most plausible reasoning could be the following. It was a few days before the annual budget. There was rumour that the country may not be holding sufficient dollar and there may be some serious announcement in the upcoming budget. As a result, banks stopped (or reduced) selling US dollars informally (there was no announcement), especially to small customers. This artificial crisis pushed the dollar price up in the grey market and regular market receives a signal from there. The question is whether government machinery is in a position to receive information and react accordingly both through policy and enforcement. I have also noted during another visit an artificial crisis of fuel due to shortage of foreign exchange temporarily. Oil ships were parked outside Dar port waiting for import bill payment. As per standard economic theory, rent-seeking behaviour flourishes during this time. Role of state and the existence of right kind of institutional mechanism and governance in this context become more than relevant. Free market economy requires the strong government more to ensure stability. Many a time, market solution does not solve a management conflict efficiently especially when losers have the capability to organise countervailing action (even politically). Ha-Joon Chang argued this lucidly in his book *Globalisation, Economic Development and the Role of the State.*

Many countries are getting adjusted fast to the global forces, and the existing institutions are also adopting the ground reality. In some countries where the value of currency is very low, the dollar becomes automatically useable currency. For example, it is very common in Vietnam, if you do not have sufficient dong in hand, you can pay a taxi driver in US dollar. In many small countries, US dollar has a ready market where buying and selling is a common phenomenon. If you travel to Macao, you will find shopkeepers willingly accept US dollar, Chinese RMB, Hong Kong dollar, and Macao pataca. Many times the situation becomes complex when the shopkeeper also returns you the change in multiple currencies. This easy conversion is convenient as the value of these currencies against US dollar is very close to each other. Vietnam manages both interest rate and exchange rate creating attractive business opportunity for foreign firms, encouraging people to invest in domestic currencies not in foreign currency and close monitoring the macroeconomic stability. On the other hand, Macao's GDP progressed significantly since it opened its casino gaming industry in 2002 and established the Free Travel Scheme (FTS) in 2003. It is growing by double digit numbers for more than ten years (especially by 27.3 per cent in 2004 and 25.3 per cent in 2007). Its currency, which is fixed against Hong Kong dollar, received a pressure for appreciation due to accumulation of huge wealth. On the other hand, Chinese RMB has been appreciated gradually, leaving Macao's pataca under stress as its terms of trade against China has been deteriorating. Macao has also experienced high inflation as most of the consumable goods are imported. As the country's trade is mostly with China, it requires its currency relation to be stable with RMB. Common citizens are also converting the domestic currency to RMB for speculative gain leading them to accept RMBs from tourists. Tourists always remain little confused with so many currency conversions and may not mind to lose few cents in each deal. Macao's macroeconomic management demands a great deal of scrutinization of its policy towards the balance between Hong Kong and mainland China.

Institutional arrangement in managing the currency in all these cases becomes very crucial, as it is difficult to measure the demand and supply of the foreign exchange and its trend daily. Cost of currency conversion in retail market can also be an issue even in a developed country. In 2008, when I was in Saarbrücken, Germany, I wanted to exchange US dollar into euro. I requested one of my students to help me in this regard as the city centre is a little far from the university. I went with him to the Deutsche Bank. It was in the afternoon. The big bank did not have many customers. Perhaps, I was the only customer in the bank. The manager ran down to meet me and asked what help he could do for me. I was amazed to see his greetings. I handed over a few hundred-dollar bills and requested him to give me the change in euro.

He went inside and requested a young lady to help him out. I was standing at the counter and discussing with my student. It was after fifteen minutes, I saw that lady in the counter call a few more people and all of them looking into the computer, throwing their hands up and down showing their inability to convert. The manager came to the counter and informed me that it would take some more time as the process is very complicated. After sometime, an easy solution came through. He asked my student to deposit the dollar in his account and withdraw euro from the ATM attached to the bank. The manager was showing his inability and also felt extremely sorry for taking time. Even in the developed economy, sometimes banking which becomes very complicated to adhere to when the processes are laid down. This increases the cost in real sense, and maybe sometimes this is necessary. Apart from this, the infrastructure and manpower also add to the cost for doing a very simple job, and I was sure that indirect cost of the banking process could be significantly high in this case. So the institutional mechanism in managing the domestic as well as international banking requires to be practical yet secured and must provide an opportunity to do profitable business. Since the Asian financial crisis in late 1990s, many countries have become extra cautious in all financial transactions whether domestic or international. This is expected to reduce different types of corruption and banking frauds. However, we have noticed that institutional mechanisms could not cope with the speed of financial innovation and small loopholes generally get noticed quite late. US subprime crisis as an example is just fresh in our mind. The challenge is to allow the institution to evolve, knowing fully that there could be possible slippage and develop checks and balance through timely intervention. Effectiveness of good governance goes hand in hand with strong enforcement of evolving regulatory structure.

As described earlier, good governance goes through good institution which can deliver good policies. After the Asian crises, it was widely discussed that deficient institutional structure was responsible for mismanagement of macroeconomic issues in many countries. WTO since 1995 has been trying to uphold good institutions in a number of sectors which has an effect on international trade such as licensing system, regulatory structure, trade facilitation, government procurement policies, etc. It was precluded in most of the common discussion that democracy is the necessary institution for developing good institutions in the country. The clean and efficient bureaucracy, judiciary system, corporate governance, information disclosure, sound financial system, etc. are necessary for good governance. After the Second World War, there was a popular argument that democratic institutions are expensive for developing countries because the functions of the democracy depend on pre-existence of good institutions. However, the world has changed, and now democracy is promoted as a precondition to develop a nation. However, many feel that democracy is more of outcome rather than the precondition for development. Hence, we are not in a position to manipulate this variable for a better development process. The experience of the democratic evolution followed different processes. We must allow developing countries to develop their own institutions considering the social norms and practices of their own culture with respect to the priorities set by the people of the country. The functioning of the democracy depends on the efficient bureaucratic system of the country. The conventional view of the bureaucracy is followed from the argument of Max Weber who feels that bureaucracy must depend on meritocratic recruitment, closed career path, and adherence to the rule-bound management system. Bureaucracy must have long-term views, and they should be generalist. However, the current policy debates are based on many reforms in the bureaucracy conducted by a number of governments which focus on an open system. This contradicts the orthodox view put forward by Max Weber. Take the example of Singapore in which the government ministries are run like corporate bodies based on specialists and their quantifiable performance. As per this view, the bureaucracy reform should be based on more short-term, open career path, and incentive-based management style. This expectedly improves the transparency and delivery system. New-age bureaucrats must be having holistic as well as specific knowledge. They should be fully gazette-friendly and have the capacity in decision-making under stress, compulsion, and against the forces of favouritism. As a researcher I had the opportunity to peep into the initial stage of a trade negotiations process. I observed that Chinese bureaucrats were very well prepared. The Chinese team consisted of young university researchers who were inculcating the real-time data, as and when it was required during the negotiations. The constant feeding of the information was helping Chinese officials in taking decision. On the contrary, the Indian team was lean, thin, and led by senior officers whose information is based on the file and 'green sheets' which were being carried by junior officers. I am sure that in many other international negotiations and talks, Indian bureaucrats are better prepared than my small experience about the system, but the aggressiveness of China is worth observing which is fully driven by the real-time knowledge base. This requires a close coordination between bureaucracy and academia. During my GTAP training in the USA, some of my peer group members were giving important interesting insights about their analysis of the Indian economy. Most of them were working closely with the government. The close relationship between academia and bureaucracy, hence, is more necessary not only to understand our own country but also about other countries. Only the ministers and very senior bureaucrats can ensure this integration between academia and bureaucrats.

Indian bureaucracy not only suffers from the inertia due to their traditional practice of maintaining status quo but also from the lack of effort to increase the knowledge base along with analytical ability. Insignificant effort is visible to develop database on a number of socio-economic issues both in central and state governments. In most of the developed economy, the data collection system required for ministries have been reformed significantly in the post-globalisation period. However, in India we still have a very archaic system in managing and reporting data. Our main concentration remains on the basic macroeconomic variables which need to be placed in so-called popular government publications. Beyond this, there is a big void or sporadic efforts. The data collection and reporting system is awfully rudimentary. In many cases, information gaps among officers are painfully huge. I remember sometime back, I met a senior officer in the West Bengal government and requested for a publication which is released regularly from his department as mentioned in the government website. He showed his surprise as he was not aware of any such publication and requested another person to enquire in the publication division. This clearly showed neither he used such an important document in decision-making nor he was interested to do so in the near future. Central government departments are only one notch above in understanding and using the data.. Some ministries which are globally exposed have improved significantly, and most young officers do use various information bases to develop meaningful notes. However, government departments which deal with socio-economic issues need to do a lot as the development process of so-called Bharat is complex which warrants continuous monitoring and analysis. Even for the smart ministries, I am sure the government does not have sufficient information. Sometime back, I ran from pillar to the post to get disaggregated data of India's outbound investment. Government was collecting and publishing the data even few years before. But latest trend is difficult to get. The common answers which I received from the officers are (1) Let me see, (2) I'll get back to you, (3) Yes, I know about such data but not sure who is in charge. The most amazing reply I received was 'What is the point of keeping such data? It is a market economy and companies are allowed to invest abroad and they are doing it.' Thankfully, RBI diligently collected the data. But someone in the government must have informed me rather than doing *bakwas* (nonsense). Many of my friends in the government have the opinion that too much data revelation to the academia and society at large may bring up insecurity due to possible emergence of loopholes; hence, there are untold common practices such as this one. However, in my opinion the days of this kind of ideas are numbered as various new practices such as citizen charter, stakeholders' consultation, and results framework documentation will eventually uphold the true democratic practices and create pressure in developing a new information base.

In late 1940s Paul Rosenstein-Rodan, analyzing the Eastern and South Eastern Europe, argued that coordination failure among complementary industries is one of the major reasons for poverty. Later on the argument gathered support, policy gap, and information gap among the implementing agencies that have been identified for coordination failure. Effectiveness of one policy depends on performance of many other policies. Interministerial policy gaps sometimes become quite costly. Having experience on working on free trade agreements (FTA), I found difficulties in mapping India's strategy towards various FTAs. More importantly the gap among Ministry of Commerce (MoC), Ministry of External Affairs (MEA), and line ministries make the internal consensus building process quite slow. This leads to several patch-up solutions (as common in coalition politics). For example, suppose MEA wants a particular benevolent FTA approach towards a country as part of India's external policy, MOC may find it difficult as India's potential gain from trade liberalization with the said country is limited but finally (maybe under pressure politically) develops a sectoral approach in bilateral liberalization. However, it is common that MoC receives jolt from the line ministry (say Agriculture Ministry) as they are more inclined towards protecting farmers' position and may not be interested in outright liberalisation. Now many views from different line ministries create a complex situation, and it is next to impossible to measure the macroeconomic impact of the deal in absence of sector-wise data. The linkage between trade and industry data is very weak, India's input-output (IO) tables are not regularly updated, and sector-wise technology developments are not imputed in IO tables. Hence, in absence of data, to run any general equilibrium model for understanding the change in dynamics of the production process due to any FTA is not possible to capture. So the impact on prices, employment, tax generation, migration, etc. is based on gross unscientific estimation. As a result, when government is finally ready for negotiation, they have unclear ideas about possible impacts of various levels of 'give and take'. India's trade negotiation always lacks a strategy space in which second and third layers of policy options are either missing or not backed by solid research due to lack of data support.

During my investigation of the Nepalese economy, it was noticed that the growth process has slowed down due to internal turmoil, and the country has been struggling to adhere to all WTO accession commitments (it became a member in 2005). Barring government officials who are directly dealing with WTO issues, the knowledge level in the government, industries, and academia are still at low level. To develop right institutions under WTO regime, Nepal government requires continuous feedback from the industries and academia. Research is required in the due course in all areas of WTO which will feed and assist the government to take right policies to handle WTO issues. Existing research capacity in Nepal on WTO area is limited. Nepal undertook twenty-five systemic commitments in its Protocol of Accession. It was granted transition periods until 1 January 2007 for implementing four WTO agreements—TRIPS (Trade Related Intellectual Property Rights), the agreement on customs valuation, TBT (Technical barriers to Trade), and SPS (Sanitary and Phyto Sanitary) rules. But by the end of the decade, Nepal remained very slow in implementing commitments and that too very sketchily. One of the major bottlenecks is the lack of capacity in the country towards developing modern institutions. The country is in great demand for developing capacity in all policy spheres. Information gap also hinders to develop right policy. Private sectors strongly feel that Nepal has good FDI policy, but it needs to improve implementation strategy and bring transparency in governing the existing policy. As the existing market size is small, Nepal should attract more export-oriented investment. Though labour cost is low in many cases, it does not help Nepal to attract more investment because of complicated labour laws and slow in skill absorption (and development). Skilled workers also migrate out of Nepal, creating a vacuum. Hence, low productivity and scarcity of skilled labour also act as an important catalyst in having low-level FDI. Initially, I got convinced by the logic of volatile trade union movement as one of the major impediments. With some more discussion at various levels, I wondered why the labour policy was not effective. It was not a big surprise that current private sectors (obviously exceptions are there) also silently support weak labour laws which suite them; hence, the pressure on the system to develop a modern system is not significant. In absence of implementation of even the existing laws, the situation quite often becomes volatile, leading to major loss of production. You may imagine similar situations in other LDCs with slight deviations in each case. Weak institutions play havoc, and countries are unable to take off even though there are signs of rising GDP and improvement of major macroeconomic variables.

Another institutional aspect is the confidence of the state to manage various conflicts. Modern and independent judiciary system is the backbone of this. Apart from this, property rights, corporate governance, maturity of financial regime, etc. are important institutions which govern the policy delivery. Ha-Joon Chang [7] argues that the role of state in conflict management should not be seen only as the ability of the state to give importance to the social or human dimension in conflict resolution but also on the economic aspects related to different dimensions of conflicts originating from different economic regimes. For example, in the post-globalisation period, treating MNCs considering the economic reality is very tricky. He argues that developing countries require a structural change in managing old institutions and developing new institutions which may call for 'creative destruction'. Without provision of a well-functioning regime of conflict management, the existing institutions will not be able to function to the fullest extent; hence, for LDCs institutional development and conflict management ability should be given upmost importance for improving policy as well productive efficiency.

5

India and the People: Uniqueness and Diversity Everywhere

In earlier chapters, we have discussed that development routes for countries vary significantly, and these dynamics are more interesting to study in case of an emerging economy. As mentioned earlier, corruption plays a very important role in defining the development route. The objective functions of different stakeholders such as government, bureaucracy, and corporate sectors may not converge into a common good. This triggers different conflicting positions which shape the development process. While talking about corruption, we have noted that some countries have organised corruption, and in some countries, it is at the mass level. Sometime back, I asked one of my friends about the difference of corruption between Japan and India. I asked that the corruption at the political level in both the countries is very high but whenever it comes out to the limelight, the Japanese minister always resigns quickly or the law takes it on course fast. However, in the case of India, neither it comes out to the limelight easily nor our legal process makes it fast enough to resolve it. While replying to my query, my friend said that in Japan, corruption is mostly centralised; hence, you can find out its chain very easily. So it is simpler to unearth a corruption compared to the Indian system where the corruption is interwoven among the stakeholders at every layer of the society. Though corruption at ground level is very common in the developing world, we must observe its declining trend as the economy moves up. However, in India it is ever increasing and affecting common people on a day-to-day basis. At the ground level, a person indulging into such activity is fully aware that he can escape with a small bribe. The credible threat against corruption has never been serious. Consumers also contribute to this, as in a growing economy the opportunity cost of getting into a small litigation is high and they always want to bypass the hassles by paying bribe. The coexistence of unique relationship between offender and corrupt officials makes the India case very special. Privileged information, close to power, capacity to create vulnerable situations for consumers, etc. are the main routes by which a common man involves into rent-seeking behaviour.

As an example on how it affects the common people, let me give you two of my experiences in Indian railways way back. I was travelling from Delhi to Mumbai sometime in early 1990s, and there was an old Parsee couple as my co-passengers. By early morning, the ticket checker came and asked my ticket. Innocently, I showed him. He did a lot of jugglery with the ticket as if he were checking its authenticity, the way we check currency notes. I was amazed to see his activity. He started asking questions: 'When did you buy the ticket?' 'Where did you buy the ticket?' I answered: 'I bought the ticket on this date and from Sarojini Nagar reservation counter.' His next question was 'What was the time of purchase?' Then he asked me why I was going to Bombay (before it was named Mumbai). As a young student, I understood that he was going to harass me for some time and, hence, got mentally prepared. When I answered all the questions one by one, he took a pause and asked me whether I could prove that my name was so and so. Remember, this was long before the days of mandatory ID card checking, which is so common these days while travelling. I had my university I-card with me, but I didn't feel like showing him at the first instance just to see how long this man could go. I acted that my name is genuine as it was printed in the records; however, he was insisting continuously and asked me to come down in the next station with him. This negotiation went on for half an hour, and I was trying to understand what his main apprehension about the ticket was. I asked him whether he suspected it as a fake ticket; he answered negative. I enquired whether my age and name was printed properly. That part was also cleared. So what was the problem? The Parsee couple then intervened and tried to tell the conductor that the ticket was genuine and that I had given reply to all the questions. The conductor asked the old couple to shut up and forced me to go along with him. I stood up brought down my diary and pen and asked his name and his identity card number so that I got to know that he himself was not a fake. I also asked the name of his supervisor. For the first time, the conductor took a back seat. I again asked, 'Can you prove me that I am not a genuine person? And if you are not able to do so, I will put you to the railway police.' I gave him three options: (1) take a hundred rupees as a bribe in front of all the passengers, (2) go to the police along with me, or (3) see my I-card and get lost. Guess which option he picked and imagine the next scene. He didn't choose any one of them and pushed himself through the crowd and left the compartment as he feared something foul.

Almost ten years after, I was returning from Kolkata to Delhi and faced another incident. I was in an AC first-class compartment from Howrah. I noticed that several gentlemen occupied my seat who were actually travelling from Howrah to the next station and identified them as professors. When the train started moving, I found an old gentleman was running and trying to board the train. I helped him to get in. He thanked me and got surprised seeing that it was the first-class AC compartment. He told me that he would travel for three hours and get down at Asansol. He assured me that he would get down in the next stop and change the compartment. Suddenly, the train ticket examiner appeared and started harassing him because he was holding the ticket of a second class. The old man politely mentioned, in the next station he would change the compartment. The so-called professors were playing cards, happily occupying my seat. They also joined the conductor and started abusing the old fellow, stating him irresponsible and a burden in the society. The conductor also threatened to put him behind bars. When the old man was baffled, the ticket examiner straight asked him to give him some money. I asked the examiner, with the same aggression, his name, wanted to see his ID card, and asked whether he had similar feelings about the so-called professors. I was sure none of them had AC first-class tickets as nobody buys it to travel for one hour only and that too in a superfast train. Fortunately, I knew few high railway officials in that route, and the name dropping worked. I told the ticket examiner, if he did not penalise others, I would inform high officers after reaching Delhi. Suddenly, everything became silent. The ticket examiner created a vulnerable situation for the old man and others who were daily free riders also had a stake to support him. In the next station when all of them got down, I tried to be friendly with the ticket examiner and asked what the compulsion on him was to behave like that. He politely replied it was the habit. Perhaps a small training from railways about etiquettes and public relation could change it. Secondly, he also mentioned that there was no credible threat on the daily passengers from railway police; hence, he could not control them.

Corruption starts in India at a very low level, and as it goes up, its volume increases significantly. Today, what we see as the protest (by Anna and others) against corruption is actually a reflection of our daily harassment which may or may not have direct political connotation always. It is not all the time possible for common people to comprehend the direct impact of the illegal deals in which officers, managers, and politicians get involved. India is a place where both organised and unorganised corruption takes place simultaneously. The exasperation which irks all of us is the routine 'rent seeking' by other common men around us only. There is no sign of abating. Perhaps, we have become very restless along with the growth impetus and, thus, contribute to the corruption as a logical consequence. We expect and demand a certain level of response from the people around us. However, the response depends on a complex process, and it does not improve overnight. Growth and civilisation move together in which synergy among variables such as education, exposure to other societies, rise in income, attempt to accept constraints and limitation of others, ability to appreciate and accept new technology reinforce each other. In our case, rising income and literacy are only two socio-economic variables which have received positive boost during the liberalisation period. Hence, it is almost impossible to expect that the other person behaves as per my expectation. So through 'backward induction' logic, the first person must behave more aggressively to start with or be mentally prepared to pay a bribe. This provides opportunity to the second person to make the situation more complicated. Suppose there is a minor road accident, and two drivers find some damage in their cars. They know that each of them would like to dissolve the matter unofficially by paying a negotiated amount. Now the question is who pays to whom. The argument starts. A possible payoff matrix in the mind of each person is given below.

		Person 1	
		Behave	Misbehave
Person 2	Behave	–1, –1	–4, 2
	Misbehave	2, –4	–2, –2

([Read the payoffs in the following way: (Person 2, Person 1) such as (Behave: Behave): (–1, –1), (Behave: Misbehave): (–4, 2)]

If both of them do not fight and accept their faults and leave the place, they may need to pay Rs1,000 each for repairing the damage. If person 1 becomes very aggressive and wins over person 2, he starts demanding higher amount, say Rs3,000. In that case, person 2 loses Rs3,000 and pays for his own damage also and, hence, incurs a loss of Rs4,000 (see the north east corner cell). Person 1 on the other hand gains Rs 2000 (Rs 3000-Rs. 1000). The entire story can be repeated for person 2 also. If he can win over person 1, he will definitely charge higher than the possible damage repairing cost. In case both of them continue the argument, police reach the place and intervene. Suppose the police also threatens and asks for bribes from both the parties. Each one of them gives Rs1,000 as bribe, and they incur loss of Rs2,000 (Rs1,000 as bribe and Rs1,000 repair cost). This is a simultaneous game, and both parties know the strategy of the other player. Carefully, see that both the players in this game have a dominant strategy which pushes them to misbehave. In other words, the payoffs in the strategy of 'misbehave' are always higher than corresponding 'behave' strategy (2 is more than –1; –2 is better than –4). Hence, both fight till the police come and end up paying Rs2,000 each despite knowing that there is a better solution as to pay for their own repair charge only. Several extension of the argument can be made from the above game which is given below.

First, when there is an argument, the demand for money as repair cost starts from a higher level such as Rs3,000, though the expected repair cost is only 1,000. If the two parties successfully negotiate, the payoffs in the north-east and south-west cells may reach to the lowest possible values such as (-2, 0) or (0, -2). If we replace the above table by these, the nature of the game also changes. Then 'misbehave' may not bring the desired result. If person 1 misbehaves, person 2 remains indifferent between 'behave' and 'misbehave' because in both the cases his loss is Rs2,000. However, if person 2 continues the argument, then police reaches. In that case, person 1's loss rises. So a vindictive person 2 will continue the argument so that the police reaches and both of them lose; otherwise, he settles the matter before the arrival of police. In that case, person 1 gains.

Secondly, how much can the police ask for bribe? From many such incidents in the past, the police are also aware that exorbitant charges from one incident will reduce future cash flow as that will induce parties to settle privately. If two parties are aware that police can ask for a hefty sum (say Rs4,000 each implying payoff as -5, -5), then 'misbehave' cannot remain as dominant strategy. Hence, the police must make a practice of demanding a rational amount, and this information will push the parties to continue the argument and also pay the bribe. In fact, if we believe that the police can actually charge a hefty sum, it leads a situation of either (misbehave: behave) or (behave: misbehave) as apparently the best strategy. However, in a loss-minimising situation, this will lead to (behave: behave). The following tables describe this. The right table explains a situation where players cannot negotiate among themselves to reduce the payment to each other, and the left table is the case where players negotiate and reduce the payment among themselves to the minimum.

		P-1	
		B	M
P-2	B	–1, –1	–2, 0
	M	0, –2	–5, –5

	P-1	
	B	M
B	–1, –1	–4, 2
M	2, –4	–5, –5

In both cases, even if we know that the police will charge a hefty sum, if P-1 misbehaves, P-2 must behave to reduce his payment. However, what is the guarantee that if P-1 misbehaves, P-2 will not misbehave? In such a situation, misbehaving will be too costly for both of them; hence, using a maxi-min strategy (to reduce the loss component), both parties rationally think and come to the solution of (B: B). Loss-minimising strategy works fine only when loss from misbehaving is very high. With plain and simple words, petty corruption thrives because the bribe amount is minimal and there is not much of credible threat. In fact only when a high degree of corruption enters, people become over-conscious and act accordingly. If the bribe is converted into authorised penalty, the police will still look for a bribe (a rational amount) and will not be interested to book the case. Hence, high penalty cannot replace the drive for private settlement. As discussed in the literature, significantly the motivation level of the police is so low that it drives towards low self-esteem and morale. Hence, they never feel ashamed to take bribes of a few hundred rupees. The image of the department also requires overhauling.

Thus, in many developing countries, focus is being given towards smart uniform, modern gazettes, and good looks. This can attract smart, intelligent young people in the department who can overcome petty issues. In our childhood, we were amazed to see how few white-dressed and mounted (on horses) police personnel in Calcutta could control a large mob or how only one good-looking traffic sergeant with white uniform, sunglasses, and his motorbike (Enfield) on the street corner was enough to discipline the unruly traffic. We used to laugh hearing the discussion between bus conductor and driver if they could see a traffic sergeant from a distance. By the way, girls were also dying to get a ride in their bike. Now the image of the police is characterised as potbellied, corrupt, middle-aged men with low morale and less tech savvy as described as *Pandu* in popular Bollywood movies in contrast to upright smart officers as *Vijay*. The police force requires regular training on technology, public relation, etc. along with their usual skill-development programmes. In several developed countries, some activities of police departments are also outsourced which include technology absorption, enhancement and related training, etc. Perhaps, to improve motivation of the force, the same is required in India.

I remember an incident of minor accident. It was in 2001, and I went to Institute of Economics at Copenhagen to attend a conference. It was early morning. The pre-winter chill was enough for me to shiver while standing on a road crossing for the signal to turn green. Suddenly, I heard a banging sound and discovered that two cars collided on the other side of the crossing. I was puzzled and could not understand what to do. The signal was still red for the walkers. Speeding cars in my side of the road were also creating obstruction for clear visibility. Smoke was coming from the cars. After a minute, I noticed both the drivers came out from the cars unhurt, but they did not talk to each other. After having a brief investigation, they picked up their phones. They had at least ten metres gap between themselves. Thankfully, the accident occurred in one corner of the road, and regular traffic was not affected much. Within minutes police and ambulance arrived. By that time, I crossed the road and came closer (obviously not very close) to the spot. The police talked to them independently; the ambulance guy did some checking and provided first aid. Once the interrogation was over, breakdown vehicles came, looked into insurance papers, and pulled the cars away. The police helped them to get a taxi for their respective destinations. During the entire incident, two drivers talked to each other in front of others for a maximum of a minute or less. How come the (B: B) solution was possible. It was dependent on many conditions as was partly discussed above. First of all, none of them expected a fight from the other, none expected that the other party would demand money, and they had trust on insurance and the police as well. In our case, for such incidents, insurance companies will also fulfil their turn of harassment.

The fear of 'moral hazard' among the insurance companies is so high that in every such case, they would like to come up as serious of riders. In my opinion, if insurance companies can cover up all expenses and provide smooth and affordable services, the bribing issues will expectedly come down in such cases.

While talking about corruption at the ministry level, common people directly relate it with the inefficiency of the government. Ministers announce projects after projects, and in many cases, they get stuck in the complicated bureaucratic process popularly known as red-tapeism. We also smell something fishy in the delayed projects, and corruption cases cannot be ruled out completely. Sometimes, corruptions are also rampant in fast-track projects. To improve the performance of bureaucrats (babus), earlier government thought of introducing variable pay for them, which were nothing but performance-linked salary. The incentive would be determined on the basis of a department's performance on predetermined annual targets. Departments would have to achieve these goals with lower administrative overhead costs to make the scheme budget-neutral. The idea is not new. It was mooted first as part of the recommendation of the Fourth Pay Commission and then ignored for decades. If departments achieve their targets, they could receive as much as 15 per cent of the cost savings. In future, this number may go up. It is expected that officials would cut costs in their own self-interest rather than being preached idealistic measures for austerity. So achieving the project target with less cash outflow is the rule of the game.

Should we think that the policy will work? It is the first step to improve efficiency and reduce the wasteful expenditure. Also this will bring motivation to officers to come out from the concept of *chalta hai* or to maintain status quo. However, corruption comes out from other angles, which is through abusing the power position to manipulate the decisions and to focus on more bribes, sometimes not in cash but in kind and facilities deriving from private sectors and citizens for which there will not be records in the government account. Babus will always have the option to get higher salary with a lot of hard work versus easy money through corruption (sacrificing a bit his/her performance-linked incentives). They can smartly maintain a middle path also.

First, let us concentrate on how the government is planning to map performance and whether the current framework is effective or pushes for more inefficiency. The newly introduced Result Framework Document (RFD)[8] is expected to solve the puzzle of measuring government performance. For a private sector, there are definitive indicators such as profitability and share price, but performance of a government department is dependant largely on complex issues concerning multiple stakeholders such as parliamentarians, citizens, private sectors, and overlapping targets of different ministries (both central and state). The RFD system hinges on departments setting targets at the beginning of each year in consultation with their ministers and the cabinet secretariat, with final nods granted by a high-powered committee on government performance. Outcomes at the end of the year are compared with the objectives, and a performance rating is assigned to ministers and their departments. The framework is divided into categories such as objective, weights/sub-weights, actions, success indicators, targets (measured in ordinal scale such as excellent, very good, good). First of all the structure is too simplistic to capture performance, and it looks like a self-fulfilling target mechanism. Babus themselves will decide the targets, weights, actions, success indicators, and finally whether achieved or not. The structure will fail to distinguish the difference (statistically, I presume) between and within [9] groups (read as ministries) as on an average, each ministry will try to showcase superb performance. Why are the most important stakeholders, such as citizens, not involved in this crucial decision-making process? Ministry can select civil society experts to discuss all these important parameters. For long, India as a country, refrained from independent evaluation of externally funded projects. Now, it is doing the same for its own projects. There are several competing agencies around who can provide evaluation. If required, government can also set up an agency to do this evaluation. This is a mammoth task to evaluate so many ministries, and we require huge manpower to do the same. A public private partnership in this regard may provide an effective solution. There are a few more issues which also require immediate attention. RFD is only focusing on the objective, targets, and outcome. It is not focusing on the processes. Many international agencies focus both on output and process to achieve those outputs which are clearly documented. Agencies monitor the process in various stages. The root of corruption lies in the process itself. Process looks into the issues such as transaction of money, favouritism, lack of integration with minor targets, and midway correction possibility. Also the views of direct beneficiary must get integrated in the system of evaluation. Several projects might have a link with more than one ministry. Suppose a bridge has been built, but the transport department is inefficient to develop public transport facility through this. Hence, the gain for ultimate beneficiary is limited. A classic example could be the positioning of metro stations in Delhi. The integration with the road department is poor in some cases, and it has added to traffic chaos (such as Hauz Khas and Malviya Nagar Station in South Delhi). Public projects (like airports or metro rail systems) and public policies like allowing FDI in retail take years to translate into reality. Hence, it is difficult to rate the outcome. It is more logical to understand the processes as intermediate targets. Also, when a government project involves multiple departments, you cannot reward few and punish others. Finally, as per basic knowledge of macroeconomics, we know that when government invests, it adds to the GDP multiplier. Hence, it is important to track how the money is being spent and on the way it embraces inclusive approach in growth dynamics. The current RFD does not have any such scope to assess. In fact RFD is diverting attention from the inclusive approach. There is no parameter on creativity of the officers in developing inclusiveness of the programmes she/he is handling. RFD may prove to be eyewash, and officers may spend more time to complete the paperwork to prove that they have achieved the targets. RFD requires wider discussion with all stakeholders and must have an objective not only to track efficiency but also to bring transparency and contain corruption.

Let us now turn to another issue in which we take a lot of pride: awesome tourism endowment that India possesses. The 'Incredible India', in some way, has suddenly taken the driver's seat to improve our image worldwide. What is the effect?

Last year, I was travelling back from Europe. It was a Lufthansa flight from Frankfurt. My co-passenger was a young British (in his twenties) who introduced himself as a musician/composer working on fusion. His focus was on different types of oriental music. With juvenile excitement, he shared that actually his great-grandfather was from India, but this was his first visit to India. With giggling face, he was describing how incredible India could be. 'I want to experience the private moment in a public place.' 'What does it mean?' I enquired. 'All of you have done at least once in your life time: peeing on the city wall. I want to enjoy that very moment, the freedom which I never got in London.' I tried to explain that India is very big and poor too, all the usual blah-blah. The young man was pricking me, 'Tell me whether you have done it or not. Maybe in the night, parking your car on the roadside. Before that you were panting inside the car and looking for a suitable place, isn't it?

I know how pathetic it is in London when we madly look for a public toilet.' I was speechless and then turned the discussion successfully on other issues.

We must know that a large number of flights to and from Indian cities are not all for tourism only; it also caters to migrating workers, software engineers, traders, and managers. In many cases, foreign tourists get the first glimpse of India inside the flight itself. As soon as the bar is open, we Indians jump on the drinks. Littering the flight following heavy drinking was not uncommon for India-bound flights. Only recently, flight operators have become very vigilant and miser in providing drinks. There are other nuisances obviously in so-called cattle classes. Once returning from the Middle East, my co-passenger shocked me when he wanted my permission to smoke—yes, to smoke. I showed my surprise, pointing my finger to the 'no smoking' light. He kept himself quiet. The flight had a stop (most probably in Muscat). I went to the toilet to freshen up. After returning back to my seat, I found that the man was smiling at me. I ignored the burning smell and thought that it could be the smell of turbine fuel as the flight doors were open for new passengers to board. After a little chitchat I slept and woke up when the flight reached Delhi. Again I saw that man was smiling. I ignored him. When I was catching my taxi, he ran up to me and asked me to wait for a while. He showed his acrobatics, how to smoke inside the flight. 'You just need two fags . . . nothing more than that is required inside the flight.' He then took a brace position keeping his mouth hidden inside his knees. 'No smoke detector will ever catch you.' Proudly he vanished in the airport. As there are no great achievements in our life and although we look for those, by disobeying public law, we get a kick. Remember, these people are neither poor nor illiterate. In fact they are more exposed to the outer world compared to millions of Indians back home. One of my American friends once told me, 'Globalisation has made certain groups of Indians very proud and confident . . . but for wrong reasons. They are expert in *jugad* and consider that as special skills which none of us have . . . this is truly incredible.'

Once a foreigner receives the 'welcome drink' on arrival, they get determined to consume more of the Indian potion. In their memorable journey, the unique experience of their interaction with drivers, shopkeepers, tour guides, co-passengers, and common men on the streets remain more vivid than Taj Mahal, Khajuraho, or Varansai, etc. or their interaction with master craftsmen. Is the reason rooted in the way we promote tourism? Perhaps the answer is yes. If we follow the five-year-plan documents, India has persistently focused on pro-poor tourism with a possibility of employment generation. For that, most of the investment has been planned for improving India's competitiveness and developing new products which are cheap and affordable. Human capital formation is also mostly in terms of achieving some numbers rather than improving the quality aspects. More careful attention towards various schemes makes this conviction clearer. For example, during the XI plan, central schemes on capacity development focuses on the number of institutions planned/sanctioned and number of certificates granted.[10] Tourism development has hardly been seen as an agent for socio-economic change. This is true that more tourists coming to a tourist spot has an immense impact on the place around and future potentiality of tourism development is a direct function of the socio-economic change. We have seen that now the government under the XII plan document has given a hint towards sustainable tourism development focusing on environment, traditional culture, rapid urbanisation, and socio-economic change. However, much damage has already been done through an abrupt growth in and around tourist spots in India. Still most of the targets that the government has set for the period 2012–2017 (XII plan) are economic in nature, as given in the table below. Ministry initiated an effort to define sustainability in 2010, following the guidelines prepared by United Nations Environment Programme (UNEP) and UNWTO. The process of developing Sustainable Tourism Criteria for India (STCI) is yet to be finalized, keep aside the practicality of implementing this.

Table 2: Specific Plan Targets in Tourism Development

Plan	Budget	Foreign Tourist Growth	Domestic Tourist Growth	India's Share in World Tourist Arrivals	India's Share in World Tourism Receipts
XI	Rs5,156 cr	CAGR of 6.79% (2006–2011), projected	CAGR of 12.49% (2006–2010)	0.6% at the end of 2010	1.54% in 2010
XII	Rs22,800 cr	12.38%	12.16%	Target 1% by 2017	

XII plan also targets creation of 2.5 crore jobs in the sector. 1cr=10 Million
Source: compiled by author from the plan documents.

India has been warned in many studies about the eventuality of uncontrolled mass tourism. In my recent visit to Ranthambhore, I was amazed to see how the truckload of tourists entered the park without proper information (dos and don'ts) which was supposed to be shared in details either by park authority or by the guide who is mostly a local person having knowledge about the forest. In fact park gates were poorly manned to cater to such a large number of tourists. Visits to a jungle should be a lesson to visitors beyond the textbook especially about the livelihood of wild animals, fragility of the ecosystem, and our duty to protect them. The nature tourism is always full of surprises, and we come face-to-face with the bounty given by the mother earth. In this case, tourists had a joy ride with a picnic mode. No one was there to check whether people enter with plastic packets, cigarettes, mobile phones (in vibrating mode), and whatnot. Nobody briefed them what tourists should not do to disturb animals. Over-commercialisation is taking its own toll slowly at Sawai Madhopur. Let me give a contrasting scenario. Some years back, my old friend Sandip at Dar es Salaam arranged a tour to Ngorongoro and Lake Manyara. Once we reached the park, after completing the usual formalities, we were introduced to our guide, a young Tanzanian. He was studying the reproductive system of wild animals in a European university. During that time, he was on a field trip. With such a knowledgeable guide, our hunger for information increased many times. We spent hours inside the park, waited for long to see how lions get ready to kill, how animals form groups to protect themselves, etc. Remember Tanzania is an LDC, yet people are proud of their national treasures and motivate others to know far more than what a usual tourist is looking for, going beyond just commercial mode. Once I asked an officer, it seemed that safaris were costly in Tanzania compared to Kenya. The answer was, in support of conservation, some types of tourism require to be expensive so that tourists also comprehend and contribute to the cause. The money must go to protect the entire ecosystem, which includes the development of Masai and other ethnic population. In India, though, there are genuine attempts to conserve forests; nobody can deny the commercial motive around the forests also in which local population get trapped. In the name of tourism, employment increases, but its sustainability is always in question as there is a possibility of deterioration of the spot itself. When you go for African safaris, you will notice different tourist products outside the forests such as boating, staying in a Masai village, artificial rope walk, and exotic food joints and balloon safari. All are mostly far from the forest and caters to common tourists. However, strict vigilance is observed while entering the forest and that too in the hand of well-versed knowledgeable guides. All such spots have clear indication of possible number of hotels and resorts which can be set up and so is for other activities. However, in India when we push tourism with employment generation and pro-poor motive only without having focus on sustainability, the deterioration of the quality of tourist spots is an eventuality. Many of the abrupt developments happened by encroaching the buffer areas. In fact when Wild Life Protection Amendment Act 2006 came into force, many state governments were in a hurry to notify the buffer areas without scientific process and public consultation.[11] Studies show that most of the generated employments for locals are in the informal sector and also seasonal.[12] High skill and managerial jobs are mostly controlled by outsiders. There has been a perennial complaint that the people who protect the forest, the earning from tourism are hardly spent on them. The sudden change in livelihoods from agriculture to tourism-related activities has its ill effect on the quality of tourism as only few of them are trained properly. The recent Supreme Court Order temporarily banning tourists in core areas of the forest (where tiger lives) is nothing but a damage-control measure rather than owning and asking governments (both centre and state) to accept the effect of wrong policies and its implementation in the past. This may be another policy stance which may hamper the normal economic growth of those areas as the socio-economic structure has permanently changed due to earlier policies. It is also warranted to enquire about the delay of preparing the Sustainable Tourism Criteria for India (STCI) and its implementation problem.

Two of my favourite weekend hideouts Haridwar and Agra are also outcomes of fallacy in tourism policy. Even ten years back, the morning/evening walk along the river Ganga at Haridwar was something which I was considering most refreshing. Haridwar was congested during that time also. But it didn't pollute the serenity. Somehow the place, I feel, has become a confluence of conflicting forces: spirituality and religious overenthusiasm. The new breed of tourists feed the economy and leave their footprints creating chaos and uncaring attitude every day. Do we have any link with the policy tools? Perhaps yes. Haridwar experiences periodic heavy rush due to Kumbh Mela. The entire attention has been directed towards overlooking the daily floating population. They remained in the hands of pro-poor employment-generating tourism policy which completely ignored the sustainability issue.

In 2007, the Asian Development Bank prepared a report on Haridwar for the Urban Development Department, government of Uttarakhand. The report not only did a situation analysis and focused on urban amenities and utilities, it also gave due importance to the tourism and heritage issues. It mentions that Haridwar lacks long-term plans for conservation of heritage spots and structures. Participatory aspects among various groups are necessary in developing the holistic plan as many places are privately owned and encroachments are rampant due to earlier 'easy go' practices. The focus requires to be strengthened towards high-end tourism, adventure, island, and nature tourism. It is important to pull the floating population out of the centre point towards other attractions. Few such efforts are now visible. A large number of unauthorised tour operators is also a nuisance. We also require few authorised tourist information bureaus which can provide authentic information and on which tourists can rely. Mushrooming of such kiosks in private hands may lead to rent-seeking activities. The literature on river Ganga and how we can contribute to its cleanliness should be developed, showcasing periodic achievements of Ganga Action Plan and other environmental projects. A glimpse of those must come under the tourism map as part of sustainability in which tourists can also contribute. Though Uttarakhand as a whole progressed significantly, Haridwar is chocked up due to its own growth and increase in tourists. Between 1985 to 2001, its residential area increased from 21 per cent to 31 per cent, parks and gardens reduced from 25 per cent to only 11 per cent of total available land in the municipal area. There has been a compulsion to increase public utilities due to heavy pressure of tourists. The area designated for Kumbh Mela has also increased from 9 per cent to 13 per cent. The paradox is all such development initiatives have tried to change land use pattern through an internal substitution among different types of usages. During IX and X plan, we should have given more importance towards sustainable tourism development and aligned it with urban development programmes. Without such effort, the growth pattern concentrated around few places in Haridwar with completely unplanned investment drive. This has deteriorated the service quality in the core tourist areas, especially sanitation. This has also polluted the river significantly as all city water eventually falls to the river. Now the cost of treating the water has increased by many folds to make it at least fit for bathing. This would have been different had it been the case we took early decision while allowing mass tourism to grow fast.

In 1993 UNESCO [13] highlighted that cultural roots must be basic and imperative in formulating tourism policy. Nehru also focused on the similar issue in his writings. Soon after India adopted New Economic Policy, the importance of tourism was seen from the economic angle (only): earning much-needed foreign exchange and providing employment. This is evident in the objectives stated in the National Action Plan for Tourism prepared by the government of India in May 1992 and in the recommendations of the Planning Commission's Report of the National Committee on Tourism of May 1988. Since then till the beginning of XII plan, relentlessly India promoted mass tourism without focusing much on sustainability (except briefly in Tourism Policy in 1982). We need to remember that tourism brings about more complex changes than other economic development projects because it necessarily juxtaposes people of different cultures and economic attributes. Also, the changes imposed by tourism are massive because it is one of the fastest growing segments of the Indian economy. The UNESCO study reinforces that a major reason for social and cultural problems following in the wake of tourism is because the tourism industry in India operates in a disjointed manner. There is a paradox also. At one side, government is too much concerned about fiscal and administrative control and on the other hand letting laissez-faire attitude to prevail at implementation level without bothering about standards, heritage protection, and impact on society and culture. Thus, one finds only perfunctory regulatory mechanism (often ignored in practice) to monitor the activities of the important 'cultural brokers' like tour operators, travel agents, guides, managers of small hotels and restaurants, and the transport agents who interact actively with tourists. The untrained, unrestrained 'cultural brokers' are more interested in making a sale, than in providing better service or husbanding the cultural resource on which their future business is dependent (mind the difference between Tanzanian guides and guides at Ranthambhore). This short-term economic perspective reflects a fragile, highly competitive business environment feeding on hyperbole rather than being derived from socially responsible action. The government's increasing budgetary provisions reflecting in more funds for training institutions and certifying more professionals have only a little impact on the tourism industry especially at the mass level. In fact a common low-budget tourist hardly interacts with trained professionals even today in India.

Through the eyes of foreign tourists when we look at India, it is 'certainly an experience. India is not a place you simply and clinically "see"; it's a total experience, an assault on the senses, a place you'll never forget' (*Lonely Planet*, 1990). It is definitely an outcome which roots both into our cultural diversity as well as lack of focus in our policy, forcing our monuments and heritage spots to become unruly oriental *bazaar*.

6

Free Trade Agreements: What Is There for Government, Corporations, and the People

I magine a situation. The room is ready for tough negotiation among member countries of a trade bloc. Some countries have large delegates, and each person has defined roles. For some countries, officers want to get connected with headquarters at home and brought several researchers, university students, and business representatives to help them during the negotiation. Those academic and business delegates are sitting in a different room with their laptop on and directly connected to home-country offices. Here come two gentlemen from India; one is a well-dressed senior officer and other one quite junior (not in age) in his crumpled suit of 1980s. They are carrying one file, with few green sheets and out of which one has proud signature of higher authority giving them the mandate to negotiate. Neither of them is carrying any laptop nor do their phones have international connection (sometime local Indian Mission provides them a phone, which does not have necessary numbers saved). Trade negotiations are difficult as it is full of numbers, codes, custom-duty rates, etc. The negotiation is for hard bargaining where a country's stake is involved. In a multiparty talk, countries negotiate for more market access in other countries but try to offer less opening of their home countries. This tug of war requires relentless calculation at the back end to understand whether we are gaining or not (at least hypothetically). The situation becomes volatile during the negotiation. Negotiating experience as well as up-to-date knowledge with continuous backroom calculations is a basic requisite for success. The situation narrated above describes the position of India even a few years back except for the WTO negotiation. India has been a slow learner and slower in implementing the experience into practice. Of course, the situation has changed, and India is now better positioned to negotiate. But the question is how much better and for what gains?

Regional trade agreements (RTA) is a generic term covering different types of agreements. Preferential trade agreements (PTAs), free trade agreements (FTAs), comprehensive economic cooperation/partnership agreements (CECA/CEPA) are the most common types of agreements which are used by countries to integrate themselves with other countries. To understand these agreements a bit more, we need to know about trade data capturing mechanism. When trade occurs between two countries, export–import and other data is captured against codes of products (Harmonised System (HS) or Standard International Trade Classification Codes (SITC)). Countries have mostly adopted HS system though several countries still follow SITC system. Under HS system, initially goods are classified in an aggregative format under two-digit levels (codes are from 01 to 99). Further, two digits are disaggregated into four-, six-, and eight-digit codes. Advanced countries have very disaggregated data up to ten-digit levels. The codes with the broadest coverage are the first four digits and are referred to as the heading. Up to six-digit level codes are standardised all over the world, and further subheadings at eight-digit level generally are considered to put tariff rates against them. For an example, HS-10 reflects the code for cereals. Under that HS 1006 clubs different kinds of rice. Below that 100610 is for rice in husk, 100630 is for semi- or wholly milled rice.

Table 3: Example of HS Structure (of HS-10)

HS 2	HS 4	HS6	HS 8	Description
10				Cereals
	1006			Rice
		100610		Rice in husk (paddy or rough)

			10061010	Rice in husk (paddy or rough): of seed quality
		100630		Semi-milled or wholly milled rice, whether or not polished or glazed
			10063010	Semi-milled or wholly milled rice, whether or not polished or glazed: rice, parboiled

When trade negotiation starts, it is always based on some list of HS codes (generally at six- or eight-digit level). As the tariff rates are placed against HS codes, countries exchange lists of HS codes in which they want partner countries to reduce duty and other barriers. PTA is an arrangement where countries mutually agree to reduce duty on some products. The list may not be the same for all countries. Under FTA, countries agree for a rule of tariff reduction over time which finally hit zero-duty after few years. To have an effective trade agreement, FTA may include different speed for different lists of products such as early harvest scheme (zero duty from the date of implementation), fast track (tariffs are slashed drastically and then reduced to zero within two/three years), normal track (tariff gets reduced gradually over medium term), sensitive list (in which a country reserves the right to reverse duty if required), negative list (generally a small list of products in which countries agree not to reduce tariff till the next review of the list). As discussed, the job of a negotiator is to push for more market access and give little in terms of committing for tariff reduction of her/his own country. Though tentative lists are exchanged beforehand, on the negotiation table, goods can move from one list to another due to bargaining. Negotiators need to be prompt, analytically sharp, have real-time information, and bold enough to push a country's position. Apart from agreeing to various kinds of lists, countries also need to agree to rules of origin (RoO). 'Rules of Origin' is a set of rules by which goods are qualified to avail preferential treatment through PTA/FTA route. These rules are based on various criteria to avoid snipping of goods originating in a non-member country to one of the member countries through another one. For example, if A and B has trade agreement and B and C has another agreement, goods from C can enter B and, having little value addition, further enter to A using the trade agreement between A and B. RoO provides clarity on this. This states that how much minimum-value addition is required on imported materials to qualify the good to be traded through FTA route. This sometimes includes rules like along with value-addition goods, much undergo change of HS subheading (four- or six-digit level). Apart from PTA and FTA, new-age trade negotiation includes mutual liberalisation of services trade and investment regime. These agreements are put under CEPA or CECA. Recently India has implemented few such agreements such as with Singapore, Japan, Korea Rep. Any agreement may also consist of some other issues such as easing of trade facilitation, dispute resolution, non-tariff measures, safeguard measures, and administrative procedure.

Let us now turn to more detailed issues. Why was the Indian government slow and hesitant to take decision for FTAs? India had experience in early 1990s the signing of South Asian Preferential Trade Agreements (SAPTA) and also a few rounds of discussion in Bangkok Agreement (now changed to Asia Pacific Trade Agreement). First time in the case of India–Sri Lanka trade agreement, the experience of SAPTA was taken to test. The biggest vacuum was found in the case of availability of related data to understand its impact on the economy. Though trade data has been available, the main issue was what would be the predicted impact on the economy as a whole. How different industrial sectors would receive the benefits of liberalization. In absence of data, the government brought out innovative methods. At first level, some researchers have been asked to do analyses who in turn worked mostly on the trade data. At the second level, industry associations were asked to come up with a wish list through discussion with their members. However, in both cases, consumers, the biggest stakeholder of the game were neglected. We utterly failed to predict its impact on prices, employment, and adjustment on the industrial sector. It was thought that Sri Lanka, being a small player, cannot have significant impact. However, in the last ten years, a series of studies reflected that Sri Lanka's exports to India increased significantly (mostly covered by the products in which it has got concession), and on the contrary, India's export increased on those products which are not under the purview of FTA.[14] During the first half of 2000, India was more focused towards the Doha Agenda of WTO and expected that it would get significant market access in developed countries if it could pursue it vigorously. However, expectation started dwindling after a few years, and then India's 'look east' policy came up as a new opportunity. But the fear of incapability to develop a good negotiating position with various scenarios and their probable impact deluged the government. It started focusing more and more on stakeholder consultation and less and less on analytical framework which requires huge data.

To understand the impact more holistically, a country needs to develop an economy-wide model (general equilibrium) as FTA is going to have an impact on all stakeholders including the government. A flow chart is given below for better understanding. Once the custom duty goes down, government revenue is bound to change. Alteration in industrial activity due to FTA also changes excise and other revenues for the government. On the other hand, due to change in industrial activities and import of goods from other countries, price and employment are also affected. So any significant move towards FTA is bound to have effect both on supply and demand of a country.

Figure 2: Trade Liberalisation and Its Effects on the Economy

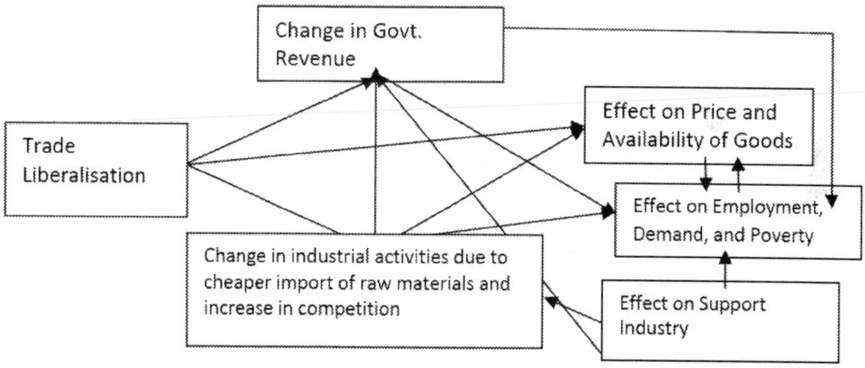

But where is the problem? In India most of the impact analysis is based on a partial model. We have also major data issues related to other variables such as industrial activities and government revenue. We also need to link supply side with the consumption pattern of individuals and employment generation. Different agencies are collecting these data for decades, but mutual coherence is missing both in terms of data frequency and also in terms of linking one dataset with others. Let us have a closer look through the table below.

Table 4: Sources of Indian Data

Nature of Data	Agencies/Source	Codes and Frequency*
Trade	DGCI&S	Based on HS codes (Monthly/Annual)
Industry	CSO	Based on NIC codes (Annual)
Custom revenue	Customs	Based on Tariff lines (HS code) but not available in public (Monthly/Annual)
Employment	CSO	Based on NIC (Annual) but not updated regularly
Employment	NSSO	Can be tracked through NIC but frequency of survey rounds are one year or more.
Technology Change	CSO (Input-output)	Based on NIC but not regularly updated
Prices	CSO	Based on major commodity groups (weekly)
Consumption	NSSO	Can be tracked through NIC but frequency of survey rounds are one year or more.

* As codes and frequency do not match and some data are not regularly updated, it becomes a Herculean task to develop a nationwide model which can be updated regularly.

Due to the existence of data gap, it is difficult to predict the outcome of any agreement. This is important to note that though trade negotiation is a responsibility of the Ministry of Commerce, data sources are lying in the hands of different ministries. Under the current circumstance it is difficult to bring all related agencies at the same platform and address the data integration issue. In absence of a robust or even a weak model, policymakers are fully dependent on loose framework to develop their negotiating position. As trade negotiation is based on several alternative options, we are unable to map the gains and losses by a qualitative framework only. This is also important to note that India does not reveal the trade data through FTA route. Hence, it is a major problem for researchers to model the FTA benefit as we don't know out of total trade how much is through which FTAs (by HS codes). More problematic is to measure the impact on services sectors due to complete absence of data. Hence, most of

India's projection is based on intelligent guesses rather than a solid analytical framework.

Let us now see how the corporate sector is gearing up to the new reality. Studies show that Indian traders largely avoid FTA routes because of operational complications. Goods face large number of queries, and sometimes certificates of origin are being challenged. A large number of traders also have astonishingly low knowledge of trade agreements. Despite seminars, conferences, the exporters and importers still remain more cautious about extra paperwork required to avail the FTA benefits. In India close to 50 per cent of exports are accrued to SME players, and the FTAs and CEPAs with Asian countries provide a new opportunity to them. However, lack of knowledge about these economies and the fear of complicated custom procedure discourage them to use FTA routes mostly. However, several big players are taking the advantage of FTA. Toyota has set up a JV accessories plant in India and has increased its exports especially gear boxes to Thailand which is a global production hub of Toyota. Interestingly, these products find a place in India–Thailand free trade agreement. CEPA with Japan and Korea have helped big automobile players get diesel-car components easily. Several Indian companies invested to set up plants in Sri Lanka to manufacture copper products from the imported copper scraps and export back to India and other countries. A study by Deloitte [15] shows that India has significant comparative advantage in exporting automotive components, textile, pharmaceutical, and chemical products and in a number of services. It is also expected that small economies in ASEAN will be attractive markets for India.[16] A survey [17] organized by Indian High Commission at Malaysia finds that the country is a potentially good market for various industrial machineries such as packaging, food processing, textile, general machinery, power generating machinery, railway and signalling equipment, etc. In fact, India's export to Malaysia in this category is rising significantly. However, SMEs should take advantage of both India–Malaysia CEPA and India–ASEAN FTA. The series of CEPA agreements with a number of countries have shown the indication of opening up of non-IT service sectors to India also. Engineering services, architectural services, urban planning, audiovisual, medical, legal services etc. are few such services where India's

CEPA partners have opened the door. These will help India's services to get integrated with these markets in the coming future.

Most of the international trade- and business-related courses in universities and B-schools also don't get into the details of these issues. In fact, the interface between international trade and marketing requires holistic understanding of both the issues. In Indian schools the synchronization of these two aspects are yet to come up as a full-fledged standard course. Some sporadic attempts must get the credit in this direction. This is important to encourage managers to look into the window of FTAs and find out the opportunities. Trade and investment help firms to generate new values both inside and outside the country. But to achieve this, they require new strategies and ground-level tactics. Trade and investment provides firms opportunity to co-opt, compete, and cooperate. Kotler in his lecture at the ASEAN Secretariat brought all such issues together which is modified for the current context and described in the table below. Companies need to take trade agreements into consideration and reorient their Strategy, Tactics, and Values (STV) accordingly. Managers of Indian companies must make themselves comfortable with this new reality and cease identifying international business just as an extension of domestic business. The nuances of international business become all the more important in a globalised world, and Indians must understand it before it gets too late.

Table 5: Interface between Marketing and International Trade: Strategy, Tactics, and Values

STV	STV Dynamics	Details of STV Dynamics	Operational Issues
Strategy	Segmentation → Targeting → Positioning	'Mapping' Strategy to 'Fitting' Strategy and then to 'Being' Strategy	**Explore** each market and position accordingly. Use FTA to enter market but position differently

| Tactics | Selling
➜ Marketing Mix
➜ Differentiation | 'Capture' tactic to
'Creation' tactic to
'Core' Tactic | **Engage**
domestic firms
to differentiate
the core product.
Use FTA to
link production
process of different
countries |
| Value | Brand
➜ Service
➜ Process | Value 'Indicator' to
Value 'Enhancer' and
then to Value 'Enabler' | **Execute** process
as value enabler
from Brand as
the value. Refine
the international
production
network through
knowledge transfer
and encourage
innovation |

Source: modified from Phillip Kotler's lecture on 'Rethinking ASEAN: Towards ASEAN Community 2015' at the ASEAN Secretariat, Jakarta, 7 August 2007.

People in India have also woken up with the new reality. We are now accustomed to see apples coming from Australia/New Zealand, FMCG products originating in Thailand or Korea Rep. We must know that such cases will be more frequent in coming days. How far are our goods reaching other countries? So far, Indian business communities mostly targeted population of Indian origin abroad, but the target customers are fast changing. We don't get surprised any more while seeing Indian textile products and readymade garments in US departmental stores. But are we doing enough? Small countries such as Bangladesh and Sri Lanka have become very aggressive in this context. Bangladesh is now a well-known player in garments. Sri Lanka has established itself firmly in exporting tea. The very word 'FTA' has produced an uncanny feeling in India. There has been a series of protests against ASEAN FTA in Southern India. The India–Sri Lanka agreement was also criticised. The India–Thailand FTA was also not appreciated in the north-east. My own assessment is that many of such protests were due to lack of understanding of FTA issues partly because of reasons discussed above. There has been coincidence of severe losses in a number of sectors such as in spices, coconut, copper products, and edible oils following the India–Sri Lanka agreement, and there is a fear that the ASEAN FTA will wipe out many small sectors. Some of such apprehensions are genuine, but how much are they due to FTA? While conducting field survey in Kerala, I have noted that

1. There is a huge gap between FTA and other policy measures required to manage post FTA situations.
2. This is due to the fact that some policies are managed by state governments who are not properly equipped; some issues are handled by other central ministries.
3. Less focus is there on productivity development and assurance minimum prices to farmers.

As an example, I can mention the fact that there was hue and cry about black pepper import from Sri Lanka. Import through FTA had a quota (2,500 ton) and also a 4 per cent CVD and complicated paperwork. Importers did not prefer FTA route; rather they found importing through Advanced General License (AGL) was a better option though there was a catch that they could not sell it in the domestic market. This import had to be processed for export only within a stipulated time period. But who cares! Once imported, Sri Lankan pepper flooded the domestic market and suppressed the prices. Once the export dates were approaching, these players bought pepper from the domestic market (at a lower price compared to import price from Sri Lanka) and quickly processed for extracting essential oil which was the final exportable product. The government failed to monitor how the pepper imported only for extraction and export went to common market and created all around distress for domestic farmers, traders, etc. The confusion in the market led to FTA bashing. There are sector-specific stories in all affected areas, and in most cases, it is not FTA, rather a host of other reasons are responsible. This is worth mentioning that the government of India has started responding to such issues. The major bottleneck is the understanding of FTA issues by other ministries and agencies. The Ministry of Commerce encourages more stakeholders' consultation to understand the issues. However, still there is lack of seriousness in those meetings or some local big players push their agenda, suppressing the voice of consumers and grass-roots producers.

At the end I would like to argue that FTA can be used as a stepping stone to develop a model for regional cooperation towards growth and sustainability. In this context, cooperation in ICT, transportation, infrastructure, technology transfer, and people-to-people contacts are essential. Post-globalisation world has made every country extremely vulnerable, and the process is irreversible. Hence, it is necessary through cooperation that we search for a win-win solution and, in some cases, through give-and-take policies.

Figure 3: Regional Cooperation Framework

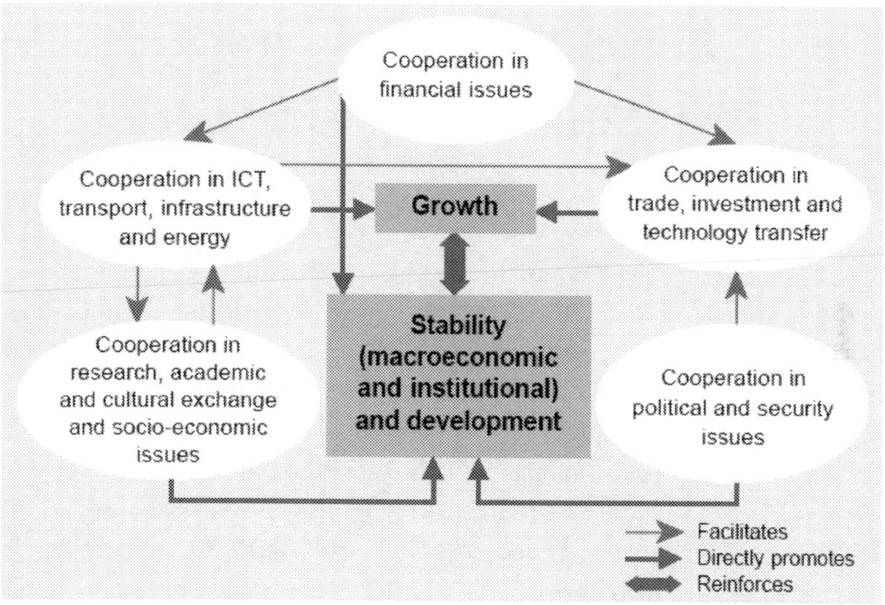

Source: UNESCAP (2004): Meeting the challenges in an era of globalisation by strengthening regional development cooperation (Figure II.1, 26).

7

Productivity and Network Development: Keys for Manufacturing Growth

I n early 2013, Central Statistical Organisation (CSO) published the data of index of industrial production (IIP) for the month of November 2012 and painted a gloomy picture. The general IIP for the month of November 2012 is 0.1 per cent lower as compared to November 2011. The cumulative growth for the period April–November 2012–13 over the corresponding period of the previous year stood at 1 per cent. In May 2013, CSO brought out the March 2013 figure which shows a growth of 2.5 per cent compared to March 2012. For the April 2012–March 2013, the overall growth of industries has been just 1 per cent. Important sectors such as metal, machinery, motor vehicles, mining and quarry, and optical instruments showed a sign of contraction. Both capital and intermediate goods have registered negative growth (–4 per cent and –0.6 per cent respectively) during April 2012–March 2013.

This has relevance in the context of the target set in the twelfth five-year plan which is to achieve average GDP growth rate of 8 per cent (reduced from the earlier target set as 9–9.5 per cent).The corresponding average target growth rate of the manufacturing sector is around 7.1 per cent. The strategy to improve India's manufacturing growth rate lies in the generation of investable resources for the sector. The twelfth plan proposes to achieve the average gross capital formation rate (investment/GDP) of 38.8 per cent. However, data on domestic savings rate (savings/GDP) suggests that it is not sufficient to fully finance the targeted investment by domestic savings. Savings of the private corporate sector to enable the achievement of target of overall savings rate (33.6 per cent) has been placed between 8.2 per cent. The average net savings from abroad will be around 3.4 per cent, making the overall savings rate as 36.9 per cent. This is important to note that investment rate was calculated on the basis of constant prices whereas savings rate by current prices. The gap will be mostly financed by FDI. However, India's current account deficit will not improve much and will remain around 3.4 per cent of GDP which states that import will remain much higher than India's exports. It is also interesting to note that the manufacturing growth would not touch 10 per cent on an average as India's consumption growth will not pick up much. In fact consumption expenditure as percentage of GDP will contract by 1 per cent; hence, India's major growth drivers will be construction, transport, and trade. It is important to note that these figures will substantially change if we are unable to control inflation and exchange rate.

The juxtaposition of these information leads one to think that perhaps the current manufacturing growth rate is abysmally low to be able to achieve the plan targets, more so given the existing exchange and inflation rate. And unless we focus on a huge foreign investment in the manufacturing sector and/or generate high savings in public and private sectors for reinvestment, the overall target of GDP growth rate is difficult to achieve. The slowing down of Indian economy has already created a negative sentiment among the foreign investors, and this seems to continue for some time.

The phenomena of low manufacturing growth is a telltale story related to poor infrastructure, low investment in capital goods, shifting focus of the skilled workforce towards the service sector (at the cost of the manufacturing sector), and monumental negligence towards innovation and backward linkages with the SMEs sectors in India. There is no doubt that with the focus on service-oriented sectors for the last ten years, desired benefits of huge FDI from countries like USA, UK, Singapore, etc. have rotated the wheel of growth in India. However, growth intensifies the demand for manufactured goods, and recent slow growth in industries is a major cause of concern especially from employment and inflation point of view.

Further, it is to be noted that service sectors are not dependent on huge reserves in land; hence, real estate issues are hardly covered in debates related to the growth of this sector. On the other hand, the criticism of low FDI in the manufacturing sector is conjoined with India's land acquisition policy with its overarching negative contour. Falling manufacturing growth, negative business sentiment, and spiralling unresolved land issues do not create any hope for positive growth in FDI in the manufacturing sector in the near future. So what is the way forward?

Western world have made attempts to resolve the land and labour issues through productivity gain. In the case of India, productivity gains are not definite. Our economy initially received a boost through investment in heavy industries. The high incremental capital output ratio (ICOR) coupled with low labour productivity was the characteristic of Indian industries in 1960s and 1970s. With the gradual focus on SMEs, the agenda was to create more employment than increasing productivity or for that matter with least priority given to technology transfer. Now, the time has come for India to look into all sources of productivity gain to give a boost to the manufacturing sector as a whole.

Let us start with labour productivity. India's education system as well as the arrangement of financing higher education has led to a bias towards engineering, MBA, etc. As a consequence, Indian working class may be clearly divided into two major groups: unskilled workers and highly skilled workers. There seems to be a missing middle of semi-skilled workers. Today, banks are ready to finance higher education required for developing highly skilled workforce but reluctant to provide loans for vocational/semi-technical courses. In countries of South East Asia and in China, emphasis has been given for equally developing the semi-skilled and skilled workforce who drive labour productivity on factory floors. The wastage of demographic dividend in terms of labour productivity has recently been highlighted by *The Economist* magazine.[18]

Productivity can also be seen as a mix of better quality input, efficient throughput, and matching value chain. Product and process up-gradation, inter-chain and functional innovations are as much important as the need for integration between the semi-skilled and skilled workers. So far, Indian policymakers seem short of this ideal. The growth of South East Asia and China are based on international production network (IPN) in which growth of total factor productivity (TFP) is achieved through the contribution of workers while integrating different stages of production further leading to up-gradation and innovation. This process gained momentum through liberalization of international trade, thereby drawing investment in SMEs which played a crucial role in enhancing overall productivity.

Production network is driven by three broad theories: fragmentation theory, agglomeration theory, and internationalization theory. Due to the fast technological innovation and rapid growth of communication, production process has vertically divided it into many stages (fragmentation), and production of each stage is now located in different parts of the world. SMEs are actively engaged in supplying parts and components with efficient delivery systems. These SMEs do not possess internal economies of scale in production; however, through government support, formation of clusters (agglomeration) is encouraged so as to create the base for an efficient procurement system for the MNCs. Thus, today's global production system reveals a unique face reflected via fragmentation and agglomeration. As production process is divided into various stages, firms require outsourcing of components. Each firm has to decide about parts to be produced internally and those that may be outsourced. The decision is also dependent on how much the firm invests in downstream and upstream supply chain to make the network cohesive or loose. This boundary setting is called internationalisation decision. India has active free trade agreements with many countries, yet it is not very clear whether India aims to overtly encourage production network.

As far as land availability is concerned, much of it could be handled with positive cooperation between Indian SMEs and their global partners. Vast acres of land are being wasted in the guise of many sick firms, especially in places like Mumbai and Kolkata. These firms can actually contribute towards reviving the growth of the industrial sector through FDI and infusion of technology.

Indian SMEs are deprived of both finance and technology. Given this, innovation gets a back seat and firms remain ill-equipped in the sphere of marketing of products or linkage with the global value chain. Japanese investors never considered India as a production base for their firms in the past. However, in recent times, several Japanese companies are focusing on localisation with the sourcing of raw material and intermediate goods from

Indian SMEs. This is an opportunity that Indian SME sector should not miss. Collaboration with the Japanese firms to induce investments and joint ventures need to be promoted. This will not only take off the pressure to acquire land as an auxiliary investment criterion but will also promote technology-driven productivity. Countries like Germany which lay emphasis on heavy capital goods are also a major investor in India. With the encouragement from the European Union, member countries from Europe are right now looking at India as a technology market, especially for clean technology, biotechnology, etc. This provides an opportunity for Indian mid-sized players who could buy the technology from Europe and develop the production network with European MNCs by supplying components and accessories and even final goods to the European market. Globally, as we have entered into the fragmented production system, efficient agglomeration of SMEs and some handholding between big/ medium foreign firms and Indian SMEs have become the needs of the hour. This will surely help in accelerating India's industrial growth.

Consequently, the need is felt for a comprehensive labour policy (for skill development) and technology policy, aligned with innovation which can change the contour of India's manufacturing profile. The key to achieving the plan target rate in India's manufacturing sector lies on productivity gain and networking with upstream and downstream firms internationally, else revival of IIP will be a distant dream. This is important to note that Indian trade policymakers can also actively participate in this debate to identify the role of international trade in enhancing productivity.

So how does a network get developed? Some clues are hidden in the history of industrialization in these countries. Table 1 below explains this in detail. Export orientation was one of the major drivers for industrialization in Japan and Korea Rep. However, ASEAN followed a dual track approach. They invested both in capacity development and improvement of export sector. Japanese FDI was instrumental for this. China's focus has been mostly on cost push through low wage and economies of scale; hence, it came quite late in the production network game. On the other hand, India's initial focus was never on export, rather on the domestic production. But slowly firms have started considering an internationalization strategy.

Table 6: Industrialisation vis-à-vis Network Theories: Experience of Different Countries

Japan	Korea Rep, Taiwan	ASEAN members	China	India
Innovation, fragmentation, export orientation, and outflow of FDI for IPN development in other countries	Fragmentation, export orientation, and domestic brand development and later focusing on IPN abroad	Dual track approach: both import substitution through indigenous capacity development by FDI and export orientation especially through ASEAN IPN	Cost push and large external economies through capacity development mostly by indigenous investment initially and then by FDI. Developing its own IPN with ASEAN now	Initial focus on import substitution and much later on export promotion. Still domestic focus is predominant. SMEs are connected to Indian and Western firms mainly. Asian FTAs pushing firms to get linked to Asian IPNs
Focus mostly on fragmentation and internationalisation	Focus on fragmentation and agglomeration of SMEs	Focus initially on agglomeration and then fragmentation and now fully on internationalisation	Focus mostly on agglomeration and now on internationalisation	Initial focus on heavy industry and now on agglomeration. Slowly moving towards internationalisation

Japanese investment flow to newly industrialized economies (NIEs) in Asia has been spectacular which has attracted many scholars to work on the subject. The famous 'flying geese' model has been developed from the Japanese style of investment. In that model, Japanese MNCs (lead goose) spend huge amounts of capital in the home country for R & D, and they also invest significantly in these countries for mass production. These MNCs also created a large number of Japanese joint ventures (JVs) in NIEs and South East Asia, which were highly productive as well as innovative. The entire phenomena unbundled the production process with Japanese precision and production of parts and components spread over different economies. The proliferation of production network has been accentuated in recent times along with various trade agreements. Lower tariff, streamlining of trade facilitation, fast movement of goods from one country to another country have made South East Asia and China truly the 'factory of the world'.

Initially, Japanese investment was limited to few countries, but it has spread to lesser developed economies such as in Vietnam. For example, when you drive from Hanoi International Airport to the city, you will cross big Japanese clusters in which both MNCs and local JVs are present. The model is more comprehensive in countries such as Thailand, whereas the government's investment policy has been aligned with the investment strategy of Japanese MNCs.

Trade between Japan and East Asia has grown significantly in 1990s. By 2000, the share of machinery exports in Japan's total exports to East Asia was around 75 per cent while import was 32 per cent. These JVs also started supplying parts and components to other MNCs. The Japanese production system initially was in the nature of subcontracting (Shitauke) or long-term relationship between large assemblers and SMEs. In mid 1980s, lots of fresh FDI made the agglomeration more cohesive, but the relationship between upstream and downstream companies remained competitive and non-exclusive ones.

Many Japanese firms are also involved in trading business. There is a clear indication of sector switch strategy by Japanese parent firms and their affiliates in East Asia. While parent firms have in general various activities across centres, foreign affiliates often conduct a narrower range of activities. Foreign affiliates are more involved in activities to participate in production and distribution network. This implies that Japanese firms have also helped in developing modern logistic chains in South East Asia.

Along with the infrastructural efficiency, Japanese firms have also focused on productive efficiency through technology up-gradation and supply chain precision. Even in India, the initial efficiency of Japanese firms is because of superior technology and their usability in production system. However, many Korean as well as European firms were able to sell their goods cheaper than Japanese goods by replacing capital by outsourcing from the local market. This has reduced not only the cost but also increased acceptability in the highly price-sensitive Indian market. To improve the cost efficiency in one of my earlier studies, I have observed that Japanese automobile companies have very little inventory time. The material comes from SMEs and goes straight to the assembly line. My obvious question was how to eliminate the defective product when there were almost zero inventories. Japanese people believe in 'no defect' and 'just in time' delivery strategies. To achieve these two, the companies have dedicated networks with the SME suppliers. Hence, all the necessary parameters of the devices along with the identification numbers were loaded in the systems from suppliers' end which are visible on a real-time basis in the supply chain department of OEM. This helps OEM to eliminate the defective material as soon as material reaches the assembly floor.[19] There are many Japanese operational innovations, like small improvements on a continuous basis (Kaizen), that are now being copied by other MNCs also. So whatever the benefits Japanese companies were getting in South East Asia, these are receding due to competition from MNCs of other countries.

Due to various reasons, Japanese find that innovation possibility is limited in India; hence, FDI from Japan has more or less constant share (out of India's total FDI) till recently. The associations between SMEs and foreign MNCs are crucial for India's future manufacturing growth and hence, Indian policymakers require more critical thinking about the quality of FDI not just as investment as numbers. India's next manufacturing growth will have to be an outcome of technological and labour productivity mix. So far government has given very less effort to link industrial policy with trade policy. In the current five-year plan, to improve India's manufacturing growth, it is necessary to develop the production network backed by a robust trade policy.

Figure 4: India needs serious thoughts in linking these policies

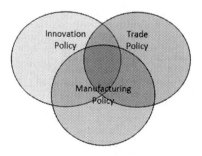

To improve India's manufacturing productivity growth, its possible linkage with innovation and trade policy requires thorough research. India's SMEs are deprived of technology and finance. They have also occupied huge amounts of industrial land (including both old and new industrial zones). The next generation manufacturing growth should come from these players. SMEs especially medium-size firms require continuous infusion of technological input which can be done through inviting more FDIs in these areas along with forcing them to be more proactive in networking. Trade policy instruments can be designed and directed towards developing international production network in some sectors along with possible joint venture development with smaller manufacturing units. The integration between trade policy and innovation policy can be thought by designing productive incentives to develop intellectual property (IP) in trade-oriented manufacturing sectors such as machinery, auto-components, electrical, chemical, and pharmaceutical sectors mainly. This will eventually increase manufacturing productivity and allow foreign firms to conduct co-creation with Indian players. The relationship of corporate sector with universities and research centres are also important in this context. As part of the foreign investment in R & D, some part of financing must go to universities and research institutions in which profit-oriented research laboratories can be developed within the existing higher education system. This will continuously feed the manufacturing sector to remain productive in the competitive world. Hence, developing a robust ecosystem around manufacturing sector with innovation and international production network is absolutely necessary to bring back Indian economy in growth trajectory.

8

Japan and Innovation: Learning for India

I t was December 2012. Temperature was below zero degree. After a five-hour train journey by Shinkansen (bullet train), we reached Kokura station. Though there are high-speed trains in other countries, the feather in the cap for Japan is that there has not been a single accident of Shinkansen so far. The flawless management of this high-speed train which carried millions of people safely in Japan is a matter of pride to every Japanese.

It was around one o'clock in the afternoon; we were sitting inside a small hall which can accommodate roughly thirty people and waiting for the lecture to begin. The room was not so impressive, but while looking on the wall and reading some of the achievements of the company, your impression is bound to change. We were at Yaskawa Electric Corporation, one of the biggest producers and innovators of robots in the world. The company started with its humble journey during the First World War as an electric-motor-making entity which diversified extensively into a variety of products in the area of mechatronics (mechanics and electronics). In 1977, the company innovated MOTOMAN-L10, the first of electric industrial robot in Japan. Thereafter, a series of motoman-s were made with refinement, and in 2003 it created SmartPal, the next-generation robot. In India, we always consider robot as competitors to humans as it can do the same work more efficiently. However,

Yaskawa's vision is about the coexistence of robots with humans. Robots are placed closely with humans to augment the skill of humans, doing complex work which otherwise is not possible manually. The new generation robot includes dual arm robots. It can also communicate and assist humans in guiding, delivering, and power assistance. As its centenary year is coming by, the company's vision has got more refined and targeted to solve global problems such as the aging society or handling of environmental and energy issues, etc. Hence, robotics is a science to be built up as human assistance in a variety of activities including the industrial sector.

During the question-answer session, I was more curious about the possibility of making robots in other countries. The company shared that eventually due to high cost of production in Japan, plants need to be installed in other parts of the world and only R & D will be focused in Japan. While visiting the factory, one particular aspect struck me about the human imagination. Any innovation is driven by the imagination, and the Yaskawa as a company gives lots of importance towards the imagination made by small kids. There are paintings by small kids who were asked what kind of job they want a robot should do and explain this by drawing. Hence, the interest towards innovation was inculcated from the school. In 1958, a picture of plum blossom drawn by the daughter of one company engineer explored the design of new motors. The petals become conductors and the centre of the flowers become the rotor. The idea of putting the conductor directly on top of the rotor of a motor gave the birth of the DC servo motor. Many engineers and scientists from different parts of the world work in the R & D department, but only a few (very few) are Indians. The example of Yaskawa provides an indication of how new-age technology is driven for developing new machines, especially in power management, water treatment, and converter devices for large-scale wind generation. The continuous ability of diversification in new areas with the proven knowledge in other areas is the key to success. The diversification through innovation has been the guiding force of the Japanese government's innovation policy to remain on the top of the world, and Yaskawa's example can depict it as a textbook case.

Japan's economy is in crisis for at least last couple of decades, as high growth of 1960s finally reached its peak and started declining since the oil shocks in 1970s. In the new millennium, Japan had struggled to reach even 1 per cent GDP growth. The growth fell into the negative territory due to the disruptions in the supply chain caused by the great Japan earthquake in March 2011. Exports are continuously declining. There has been a deflation in the prices. Recent forecasts inform that GDP in 2015 will be much smaller than the GDP in 2010. Japan is also experiencing socio-economic problems related to reduction in birth rate and increase in aged population. The bank is not providing any interest income and so is salary which also remains stagnant. In this economic structure, it is now essential for Japan to re-look at the history of its growth and work in a new direction. The only way out is to invest more on innovation and export those products giving higher commercial benefit to the people and to the nation. In the innovation world, Japan faces steep competition from other developed worlds. The sunk cost for R & D is very high, and as a result, some of the risks part is either covered through higher pricing and intellectual property rights (IPR) or by government subsidy directly. In Western developed countries, venture capitalists and angel investors remain very active to finance innovation, and most of the companies have taken up open innovation as a strategy to mitigate risk. Open innovation is the use of purposive inflows and outflows of knowledge to accelerate internal innovation and expand the markets for external use of innovation, respectively. This assumes that firms can and should use external ideas as well as internal ideas, and internal and external paths to market, as they look to advance their technology.[20] In the case of Japan, innovation is more controlled, financed, and promoted by the government in which private sector plays its role in developing the product. The role of the private company is mainly to convert the innovation into a commercial venture and making it popular globally.

During my visit to Japan, we were exposed to some such efforts by the Japanese government in collaboration with the local government. One of such products was the Kitakyushu Eco-Town Project. Kitakyushu is located south of Japan, and it prospered as an industrial city built on the backbone of the manufacturing sector. Geographically Kitakyushu is close to many big cities in the world such as Shanghai, Beijing, Seoul, Tokyo, etc. which helped the industries to sustain themselves for decades due to robust international demand.

Kitakyushu and its vicinity are considered as one of the four major industrial regions of Japan. It played a pivotal role in the modernization of Japanese industries and rapid economic growth of Japan. Unfortunately, such thriving industry led to severe pollution problems. In the 1960s Kitakyushu had the worst air pollution and waste water from factories pouring into the Dokai Bay, turning the waters into a 'dead sea' nearly devoid of life.

The first people to take a stand and demand something be done about the pollution were mothers concerned about their children's health. Residents' actions and media coverage helped spread awareness of the problem and prompted corporations and government to strengthen anti-pollution measures.

The efforts of corporations, government, and the public working together in unity led to the rapid improvement of the environment. In the 1980s Kitakyushu was introduced throughout Japan and abroad as a miraculous city that successfully restored their environment.

Table 7: Honours, Awards, and Accolades Received by Kitakyushu City

1990	Received the Global 500 Award from the United Nations Environment Programme (UNEP); a first for local government in Japan
1992	Received UNCED Local Government Honours at the United Nations Conference on Environment and Development held in Rio de Janeiro, becoming Japan's first and only recipient of the accolade
2000	ESCAP Ministerial Conference on Environment and Development in Asia and the Pacific held in Kitakyushu
2002	At the Johannesburg Summit, Kitakyushu initiatives were included in the Sustainable Development Plan of Implementation, as a model practice to promote inter-local government support
2006	Dr Wangari Muta Maathai (Nobel Prize winner) 'Kitakyushu, an Environmental Model City'
	Time, a leading US magazine, introduced Kitakyushu as a model city for environmental improvement

Source: brochure on Kitakyushu Eco-Town Project, March 2011, published by the Office of Environmental Future City Promotion, Environment Bureau, City of Kitakyushu.

Since 1971, a major project has been launched in Kitakyushu which was aimed to develop a comprehensive range of initiatives including education and basic research in the environmental field relating to technology development and demonstration research and commercialisation through cooperation with the Kitakyushu Science and Research Park. In the environmental industrial complex, there are set-ups like plastic and pet bottle recycling, office equipment recycling, automobile recycling, etc. Now, interestingly, throughout Japan, the government identified industrial zones and provided incentives to environmental industries as well as research institutions to cohabit in the same locality. Like SEZ, the government has promoted several concepts like comprehensive special zones (CSZ), future cities, etc. in which collaboration and cooperation with local authorities, medical institutions, education institutions, research institutions, and agricultural cooperatives have been made along with industrial projects. People were encouraged to be part of these innovation projects, listening to several experimental regulations imposed on them. For example, managing the domestic waste, managing the electricity, and using eco-friendly and low-emission vehicles as part of bigger experiments have been the key to success to Kitakyushu projects. There was a successful experiment by a series of companies in recycling of waste water and seawater converting into almost drinkable water which is now being reused by other industries such as in power generation. High-level RO systems have been imposed in the Water Plaza in which big Japanese MNCs have also taken part. While talking to officials at the Plaza, we gathered the information that the bulk RO system can clean the entire city sewerage water. Continuous research on the membrane to clean water has made it successful. In the future, they will make attempts to replicate the system in other Japanese cities and finally will develop its commercial aspects to be exported to other cities in the world including China and India.

Experimental smart community in the field of energy is also in an advanced stage to become more commercial and almost ready for export market. The electricity management system of Kitakyushu smart community has been divided into main four categories:

a) CEMS (Cluster Energy Management System)
b) HEMS (Home Energy Management System)
c) BEMS (Building Energy Management System)
d) FEMS (Factory Energy Management System)

An innovative small metre is about to get launched in the commercial market. These small metres will help Kitakyushu to concentrate on dynamic pricing systems of electricity. As an experiment, small metres have been installed in 230 households in which household members get information on demand projection based on past data, temperature of the day, and other information. This will help households to reduce or increase power consumption and thereby save electricity. The pricing system has three levels—basic pricing, real-time pricing, and critical pricing. The Kitakyushu officials want to convert consumers into 'prosumers' (producers and consumers) which means that when one household saves energy, the other household can use that. This indicates that there will be a credit point for energy saving.

The entire story tells us that the modern Japanese economy is making an attempt to encompass the people-centric innovation strategy which is not only going to help them to save resources or to use it optimally but also can provide a global solution in all these issues. The involvement of the common people as well as the knowledge level is impressively high in Kitakyushu which I understood while interacting with the people. The concept of cooperation and co-creation driven by the government, several stakeholders such as local authority (municipality), the community welfare board, the city-level public utility companies, small or big private sector players, and above all children play a very important role in making this project successful. Hence, community based innovation and its commercial dimension can be of big learning for the rest of the world. The incentive structure to fuel the innovation in the eco-town is also unique as it is divided both for entrepreneur and researcher. The government bears part of capital cost for entrepreneurs, but major grants are offered for researches which are divided into practical research, social system research, field survey research, etc. An example of incentive structure is described in the table below.

Table 8: Support System for Enterprises/Individuals in Eco-Town

Subsidy to Support Enterprises Doing Business in Eco-Town		Subsidy for Research and Development	
Title	Special Subsidy for Business Cluster in Special Zone for International Logistics * Subsidy options are subject to change in the 2011 fiscal year	Title	Future Environmental Technology Development Aid
Establishment Requirements	To receive the subsidy, the enterprise must have launched construction work to establish a new/additional facility in the revitalization priority area of the special zone or concluded an agreement to lease a facility in the area, during the period from 1 April 2008 to 31 March 2011. Also the facility must have started operation by 31 March 2012.	Potential Applicants	*Practical research*: Individuals who conduct R & D in the Kitakyushu Eco-Town Practical Research Area or individuals who conduct practical research in Kitakyushu City with a valid reason why they do not conduct the research in the Practical Research Area. *Social system research*: Small/medium-size enterprises that have offices (including research institutes) in Kitakyushu or individuals who conduct R & D mainly in Kitakyushu, in cooperation with enterprises located in the city. *FS research*: Small/medium-size enterprises that have offices (including research institutes) in Kitakyushu or individuals who live in Kitakyushu and conduct R & D in cooperation with enterprises located in the city.

Eligible Industries	Manufacturing (including recycling facilities) and others			*Practical research*: Research and development of a socio-economic system, in which material procurement and logistics play important roles for development of the environmental industry, to establish recycling-based economic and low-carbon societies.
Investment Requirements	Large enterprises: More than 500 million yen Small and medium-sized enterprises: More than 250 million yen	Enterprises that have purchase industrial sites in Kitakyushu are exempt from investment and new employment requirements	Subject Areas	*Social system research*: Research and development of socio-economic system, for the creation of a recycling-based economy, including the procurement of important materials for the development of environmental industries and commodity distribution.
New Employment Requirements	Manufacturing: More than ten employees Non-manufacturing: More than five employees			*FS research*: Survey and research of technologies, marketability, and cost efficiency as the step prior to practical research.
Subsidy Rate	(1) Acquisition of property: [New construction] 5% of capital investment including land cost (10% for purchasers of industrial sites in Kitakyushu) [Additional construction] 3% of capital investment including land cost (6% for purchaser of industrial sites in Kitakyushu) (2) Lease of property: Half of the annual rent (first year only)	Subsidy Rate		Up to two-thirds of research expenses are granted to research projects conducted mainly by small/medium-size enterprises in Kitakyushu or to joint research projects conducted by educational research institutes and small/medium-size enterprises. Up to one-third of research expenses are granted to research projects other than the above. (For research projects in priority areas, up to half of the expenses are granted.)

Maximum Amount	1 billion yen for the sum of 1 and 2 above	Maximum Amounts	Demonstration research: 20 million yen/year (up to three years) Social system and FS research: 2 million yen/year

Source: brochure on Kitakyushu Eco-Town Project, March 2011, published by the Office of Environmental Future City Promotion, Environment Bureau, City of Kitakyushu.

India is slowly emerging as R & D centres for both large- and medium-sized MNCs in various industries. The development is mainly due to the availability of skilled labour produced by elite institutions of the country. Though cost advantage played a major role, India itself also provides a big market for innovated products. Rising income level of India and the billion-plus population are offering unique opportunities for both domestic and foreign firms who are engaged in innovation. Nevertheless, India faces major challenges related to infrastructure, bureaucratic hassles, and a major gap between the knowledge and practice. Since the last few years, the government of India has become proactive, and effort has been taken up to give the National Innovation System a shape especially during the eleventh five-year plan.

India's innovation policy has embossed the inclusive strategy in which focus has been given to innovation at the grass-roots level and encouraging SMEs to conduct process innovation. This follows rightly with the basic hypothesis as described above. India is a developing country; hence, incremental innovation is more important than investing on the major breakthrough.

The National Knowledge Commission (NKC) report 'Innovation in India' (2007) identifies the general trend in innovation and innovation strategy for India. It believes that innovation thrives in competitive environment and, in turn, places huge importance to the achievement of such an environment. Innovation generates economic values, new jobs, and new dimensions of entrepreneurship. So far we have noted that like other developing nations, India's basic investment in innovation comes from the government, especially in universities, technical labs, and dedicated institutions. However, the major lacuna lies in the commercialisation of the innovation. The 'Innovation in India' report identifies that the percentage of revenues derived from products and services which are less than three years old (innovation intensity) has increased for large firms and SMEs. As per the sample survey by NKC, 17 per cent of India's large firms linked innovation as the top strategic priority now to survive in the competition. Almost 76 per cent of firms invested in innovation as they considered incremental innovation as a major strategy, especially in one to three years time frame. However, it was noted that most of the innovations are nothing but *fine tuning of internal process or operational innovation in formalising business process into a more systematic approach*. Though NKC admits that innovation has started contributing to the economic progress in India, critics identified that it has happened mostly in a few sectors such as IT, biotechnology, etc. If we have a broader definition of grass roots which largely work through *improvisation* and *experimentation*, we can consider that this has increased significantly even in firms located in rural areas. The firms who are at this level suffer largely due to lack of information on market opportunity and limitation of capital which reduces the risk-taking ability of the firm. The early stage funding required for grass-roots innovation is extremely critical at this moment in India. If we go back to the history of Japanese innovation system, we must note that the initial innovation part happened in the SMEs sectors only, and the government played a very critical role in funding the innovation. Though we know that the deep pocket of the Japanese government is mostly responsible for the success of innovation and this has helped companies handle the gestation gap, the milieu among universities, local government, and common people have also been the driving force for success. In the case of India, the government has so far arranged some fund, but systematic approach is grossly missing. Hardly state-level universities/engineering colleges receive research directives and collaboration opportunities with private sector and local government (with few exceptions). As a result, the gap between theoretical research and commercial capability is not showing any tendency to come down.

India's approach towards *incremental innovation* is nothing but *productivity* enhancing across the range of firms, and in this context, economic externality occupies an important role. Developing industrial clusters, arranging big machines required by the small players jointly (such as leather affluent plant) are extremely critical to enhance the productivity. Sometimes countries import emerging technology without understanding its absorption capacity in the economy. This becomes quite costly as mentioned by many scholars including Prof. Amartya Sen in his writing 'Choice of Technology'. A developing country might have a wonderful ecosystem to develop theoretically a new product, how far the performance frontier of the new technology can push the price frontier is a question often asked. This is important because the price of the product needs to be affordable in the country where the innovation took place and there exists a large demand. Unfortunately, many developing countries are unable to handle this particular situation. Another important issue is about the intellectual property rights (IPR) of the invention. Often Bayh-Dole Act in the US is quoted for providing IPR protection to universities even when the product was publicly funded. The legislation has decentralized the control of federally funded inventions, vesting the responsibility and authority to commercialize inventions with the institution or company receiving a grant. As a result, it becomes easier for researchers to work in a project publicly funded with an additional opportunity to make it commercially viable (taking IP rights) with assistance from private players. As a result, PhDs and post-docs are having direct contribution to make the innovation more realistic.

During my visit to Japan when I enquired about the eco-town and other environmental projects in which private players are actively involved, it was not a surprising reply from the Japanese expert that most of the big innovations are funded by the government and co-opted by the private sector. This increases the knowledge base of the private sector, and they, in turn, try to commercialize the entire project in other parts of the country as well as outside Japan. So in the coming days, Japan will focus mostly on exporting of eco-friendly technology, especially in energy, automobile, water treatment, recycling, etc. Japan would be ready even to replicate entire eco-town project in other cities of the world. For example, if the Delhi government provides Japanese to set up the eco-town around the city to clean out garbage and wastage to save energy, then we have to buy Japanese technology to set up the project. Hence, Japan can recover the R & D investment conducted by the government. So gradually, Japan will move away from smaller innovations in FMCG and machinery products to bigger innovation with higher value and longer time span for maturity.

India though being in the lower strata of the innovation ladder has started tightening its IP laws. However, not much of investment is deriving for IP based innovation in India. The importance of venture capitalists and angel investors are very much noteworthy in this context. In India, most IP is created by either research institutions or offshoots of research institution, but commercial exploitation of these IPs is relatively less. Over 80 per cent of India's research is public funded, but it was never a public-private partnership in true sense as we saw in case of Japan. Doctoral students or other researchers both in public and private universities in India are hardly linked to a product or process development serving company's interests. The National Knowledge Commission in its 'Innovation in India' (2007) explained the need of systematic reform with a focus to the innovation ecosystem. In the system, stakeholders such as government, firm, research laboratories, universities, and financiers are connected through a comprehensive regulatory and incentive structure. The following diagram explains this. However, one of the critical issues which can improve the efficiency is about the direct connectivity between venture capitalists, firms, and innovators. In the modified diagram, these players linked with the dotted lines. Two highlighted groups—innovators (suppliers of innovation) and financiers/risk takers (demand creators)—must come together to make the Indian system more robust. Creative freedom to faculty and researchers, possibility of setting up centres and profit-oriented research laboratories within the university system partly funded by the government can work as long-term incentive.

Figure 5: The Innovation Ecosystem: Modifying the idea of National Knowledge Commission

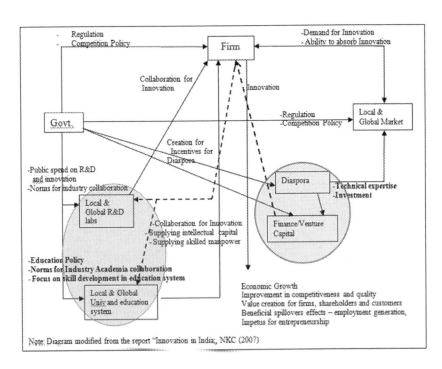

9

Africa: The Rise of *Rafiki*

I t was an early morning at Dubai airport. We were in transit, travelling from Tunis to Accra. The gate was still closed. Sleepy kids occupied the place; some other passengers just reached having a red-eye flight and trying to identify cosy seats. The place was otherwise quiet, and a large number of passengers were reading newspapers (not on phones or tabs). The attire of both men and women attracted me as they seemed to be quite costly and carefully chosen. Even the handbags and accessories were of reputed brands. I talked to my colleague, as this gave me a signal to map the culture and style sense of upwardly moving people of the country. In the flight, I got introduced to several co-passengers, including few professors from Europe who were going for a conference. While talking to people from Ghana, I had a nice and pleasant feeling as most of them were quite conversant and knowledgeable about global issues, be it environment, social uprising, global politics, or financial crisis keeping aside their interest in football and Hollywood. We had quite an intellectually stimulating discussion during the long haul of the flight.

Accra, capital of Ghana, is a nice colonial city on the Gulf of Guinea in West Africa. Ghana is one of the most stable countries in Africa and having relatively higher per capita income (more than India). India is a popular country, and Indians are respected at least in the city of Accra. Many government officers and corporate managers visited India for education, and Ghana has taken full advantage of India's ITEC (Indian Technical and Economic Cooperation)

Programme offered by the government of India. During our visit to GIMPA (Ghana Institute of Management and Public Administration), we appreciated the level of academic standards and integrity of the institute. India has close political and economic ties with Ghana. In 2010, a MoU was signed between India and Ghana for setting up a US$1.2 billion joint venture fertilizer project. The MoU on the government of India's financial and technical assistance of approximately US$0.86 million to the India–Ghana Kofi Annan Centre for Excellence in IT was signed in 2011. Despite such close government-to-government and people-to-people connections, in my understanding, we are moving quite slowly to reap the benefit of our close friendship.

India's exports experienced a leapfrog growth in recent times, and in 2012, it was close to US$800 million. India exports technology and knowledge-based items to Ghana such as pharmaceuticals, which are meant to bring down the cost of life-saving drugs and equipment. Other major exports from India to Ghana include telecommunication, agricultural machinery, electrical equipment, plastics, steel, and cement. However, India's import is only US$300 million. Ghana is one of the world's biggest producers and exporters of cocoa, and close to 70 per cent of India's import from Ghana are cocoa and related products only. It is important to note that Ghana has significant mineral deposits. The mining industry in the country accounts for around 5 per cent of the nation's total wealth. The country has significant deposits of gold, diamond, and bauxite. Ghana has recently discovered huge oil deposits in the country. One oilfield is thought to contain at least three billion barrels of oil. India, being a resources-starved country, must look for opportunities to access the mining areas of Ghana for its long-term benefit.

India's attitude towards Africa is still very traditional. Since the India–Africa Forum Summit in 2008, Africa has become a buzzword in the government circle. It has a spillover effect on industry associations, public sector enterprises, and the corporate sector at large. However, even after a few years of vigorous efforts, our engagement with Africa is less than optimal. One of the major barriers is the mindset about Africa. Most people still consider Africa a 'dark continent', a group of poverty-stricken and war-trodden countries having some of the dangerous places on earth (better not to travel there). Due to this feeling deep inside, our approach towards African nations takes a different turn. I had the opportunity to listen to some of the talks on Africa here in India. Most people from the government and corporate sector feel that Africa needs assistance, and our investment in pharmaceutical, technology, education, etc. will help them to stand up; hence, we must be allowed to enter and do business, and this will provide a win-win situation both for Africa and India. I don't believe in this approach. Today's Africa is much closer to a developed world, and they get the best assistance in many areas. Yes, we can provide a south-south solution which is cheaper, more apt for developing countries, but that does not give a special position in the mind of Africans. India must take 180-degree opposite approach. It is predicted that in another ten to fifteen years, India will face severe scarcity in food, energy, and mineral resources. Hence, India needs an efficient source for food, resources, and energy security. Africa provides enormous potentiality to help India in this regard. So rather than helping Africa, our approach should hover around to get help from these countries for our own economic security. To get resources efficiently, we require skilled and healthy African labour force. Our investment in education and health in African nations must be more specific to enhance labour efficiency both in production and services, and this also includes enhancement of systemic and managerial efficiency especially in supply chain, financial market, IT and Telecom, and streamlining of licensing and trade barriers. As most African countries have started growing recently, they are able to grab the best possible development models as suggested by international organisations. These models have already been tried, tested, and refined in other parts of the world (mainly in Asia and Latin America). So Africa is destined to address developmental conflicts in a much better way than other parts of the world. The only major gap is the financing of the process including investment in infrastructure, production, and services. So India must develop a long-term strategy based on cooperation and mutually accepted route. It must make strategic investment and secure early access to specific sectors so that our future needs are met. Secondly, due to higher income and growing consumerism, Africa will be one of the biggest markets in the near future. Indian companies especially in FMCG sectors must make an early move and streamline the local supply/value chain to respond to the consumer choice.

Figure 6: India–Africa Strategic Partnership

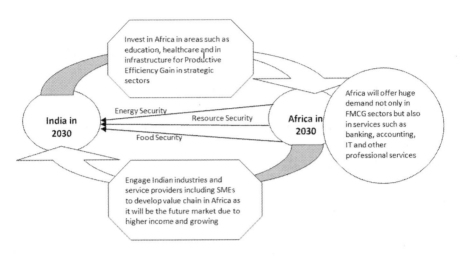

During 1980 to 2010, the growth of Africa's middle class has been fantastic. As per African Development Bank (AfDB), it consists almost 34 per cent of Africa's population in general during 2010. Africa's middle-class growth has outpaced overall population growth. Furthermore, growth of the working-age population and the high rate of urbanisation in Africa are expected to contribute to the rising middle class. Following the report 'The Rising Middle Class of Africa',[21] some North African countries have close to 80 per cent population in the middle-class bracket while the figure is above 40 per cent in West and South Africa. The African middle class is a consolidated segment, with small families, high spending, considerable savings, and access to major consumer durable goods, private health care, and education. The upper middle class spends around US$10–20 per day (2005 prices) while the lower middle class spends between US$4–10 per day. African middle class have started consuming non-essential goods significantly. AfDB predicts that though South Africa and Nigeria will lead the consumer revolution, growth of consumer spending of many other African nations will be exponential. The combined effect of poverty reduction and middle-class expansion provides huge potential for greater spending in the consumer goods market. However, this needs to be kept in mind that African market is heterogeneous and highly segmented due to income as well as cultural differences. Many foreign companies extend their products in the African market without any substantial change. However, whether it is in Accra Mall in Ghana or Shoprite in Tanzania, slowly companies have started giving preference to consumer choice. I wondered to see African dresses or utensils (of local style) made by Indian companies. Indians have a distinct advantage as they are present in this part of the world for a few generations. We can beat the distributional-channel-related problems in Africa better than any other country (I bet) due to deep penetration by Indians in almost all sectors. Domestic Indian companies having an aspiration to get a market access in Africa can easily do this provided they are able to establish contacts with Indian citizens or people of Indian origin settled there or vice versa. However, so far very little effort has been taken up to develop this coordination. Very few Indian Missions abroad have developed such strategy to connect Indians to leverage the business opportunity. As a result of this, small FDI from India in these countries are almost absent. Only large Indian players are present who can absorb the business risk in a much better way. Hence, to reap the benefit of a growing African market, India is required to have a strategic thought on how to engage and prepare Indian SMEs for the African market. I remember, one student in Tanzania enquired about the machines to prepare oral rehydration powder/salt (ORS) and to whom he should contact in India. Stupefied as I was, I could not give any reply and politely requested him to contact Indian High Commission and some business chambers in India. This guy had all the contacts with the pharma companies, but he wanted to be in touch with the machine makers. A dedicated service portal (maybe chargeable) is required linking embassy, industry association, local chamber of commerce, etc. which can throw a variety of information about the burgeoning African market. India must establish itself in the mind of African consumers especially in food, electrical, chemical, textile, and other FMCG good sectors. So far, it has done a fairly good job in pharmaceutical, automobile, metal, and machinery sectors, but other areas also need urgent attention.

While interacting with business community and government officers at Tunis, we discovered that India is still not at the top of their mind in terms of business. Tunisia being a francophone Arabic country is much close to Europe and rich Arab nations. As mentioned above, a large middle-class community is unfolding a huge demand there, which is being fed by Europe and now increasingly by China. Mr Ben Arabia Malek, one of the directors at Centre de Promotion des Exportations (CEPEX), while sharing the nature of participation in various expos, informed us that only a handful (or none sometimes) of Indian companies go to Tunisia for promotion. However, many intellectuals and corporate managers feel that Tunisia must learn from India about the global business strategy of Indian IT companies. The country has very high literacy rate, and there is no dearth of skill as technical education has been the top priority since 1956. By mid 2000, all schools in Tunisia are connected with the Internet which gives them an early mover advantage in the developing world.

Table 9: Evolution of ICT Infrastructure in Tunisia

Year	Infrastructure
1984	• Creation of the INBMI (public Internet service provider + maintenance + training)
1985	• Beginning of generalizing the use of computing in educational institutions
1988	• Internet for All project
1990	• 100 secondary schools equipped with computer labs • Office automation training programme for teachers
1998	• Connection of 30 per cent of the institutions • 1,000 teachers had free Internet and email accounts
2000	• 100 per cent of secondary schools connected to Internet
2001	• The president ordered the connection of all educational institutions to Internet and the introduction of ICT in education • All high schools and research centres connected to the Internet
2002	• Launching of the Tunisian Virtual School
2003	• The Virtual University of Tunis established as a government initiative
2006–2007	• All primary schools connected to the Internet • 20 per cent of courses offered through e-learning

Source: Amr Hamdy (2007): ICT Education in Tunisia; http://www.infodev. org/infodev-files/resource/InfodevDocuments_434.pdf.

Tunisia, being geographically close and in the same time zone of Europe, has a natural advantage to become a BPO centre for the European countries.

However, IT and IT integrated business requires not only technical skill but also managerial ability and the capacity to move from low end to higher value-added services. Many Tunisians are dying to know how India has acquired the skill and how it innovates in the business application part. This provides a wonderful win-win situation both for Indian and Tunisian industries. So far, French and Arabic languages have become one of the biggest barriers for Indians in such countries in North Africa. Indians never wanted to go to an unbeaten track and, hence, never felt to venture into this territory. Tunisians have a perennial complaint that Morocco, having comparative advantage in similar goods, is taking the lead, and Tunisia is unable to convert it to business opportunity despite having quality products and services. Olive oil from Tunisia is hardly known to India. Since the last few years, companies are trying to compete with European players. However, unless the users are aware of its quality, the usage quantity will not increase. Five Tunisian olive oil producers (Carthage Olive Oil, CHO Group, Hikma Oil, Abou Walid Group, and Huilnord Huilerie Carthaginoise), led by the Packaging and Conditioning Technical Centre (PACKTEC), participated in the Annapoorna World of Food fair in Mumbai during November 2011. Since then, these companies are making their best effort to increase the sales. This is noteworthy that Tunisian olive industry is facing perennial problem and Indian technology as well as product development strategy may come in handy for the industry to revive. Plantation, harvesting style, extraction procedure, packaging strategy, etc. require revamping. More importantly, Tunisia exports mostly unbranded oil in barrels to Europe which get branded and re-exported globally. Hence, Indian food-processing giants may look into the opportunity in Tunisia for branding the product with due value addition and diversification. We were informed that Tunisia is also not able to get due benefits despite having beautiful tourist spots. Carthage ruins showing beautiful architectures of Greek and Roman period on the Mediterranean Sea, beaches like La Marsha, Hammamet, white-blue typical buildings at Sidi Bou Said, Byzantium Roman cultural centre at Sbeitla, and the Capitoline Temple are among the finest tourist spots in the country with much less than optimal number of tourists. On the contrary, Morocco has successfully converted Arabic and Mediterranean culture into a commercially viable product with due marketing and promotion. For example, the Bollywood movie *Ek Tha Tiger* promoted Morocco to Indian tourists to a large extent. Tunisia got the boost after the shooting of *Star Wars*, but it requires more promotion to new-age tourists from countries such as Japan, China, India, etc. Indian tourism companies can occupy this vacant position, integrating the tourist spots with the potential tourists worldwide and especially in Asian region.

Above examples, indicate that India requires carefully orchestrated strategy for Africa. It is hardly possible to draw strategies for each and every African nation at one time; hence, it is better to start with important nations first—be it resource rich or transition economies or offering large demand due to growing middle class. Countries in which India has large exports, which shows higher growth, and in which India has specific interests should be identified first for this purpose. Naturally bigger markets such as Nigeria, South Africa, countries with higher demand of Indian products such as Kenya, Tanzania, oil-rich countries from West Africa, other markets having potential demand of Indian products and services such as Egypt, Ethiopia, Ghana, Morocco, Tunisia, and Sudan may be selected to develop (country X product) matrix.

Telecom companies like Airtel made a giant entry in a number of African nations. Many African banks run their process through the Finacle software. Reliance has taken over GAPCO and has a big share in the East African petroleum distribution and retail market. Three-wheeler scooters are fondly called as 'Bajaj in many African countries. Along with these, NIIT and other Indian higher education institutes' presence in Africa have made a renewed interest about Africa in India. However, the bigger question is whether these investments are pushing us close to resolve our future economic insecurity as described in the beginning. So far, we are unable to establish the link, but now there are enough information and we as a country must map the gain from such endeavour. Once a Ugandan high commissioner told me that Indians' presence in East Africa is overwhelming but not unchallenged. India requires to do more to remain in the top of the mind of the local people. I have also observed it in many parts of East Africa. People are not able to connect with the benefit of a super computer received from India as it is not visible, but a football stadium from China has a much deeper impact. Our strategy is to use India's skill in soft power, but we are culturally miles away from the locals and unable to touch their hearts, and therefore, the soft power strategy has a suboptimal outcome. Indian workers from reputed private infrastructure companies may be building roads close to Arusha or Ngorongoro, but their contacts with local Masai could be almost negligible, whereas companies from

Denmark may directly and indirectly get involved with another organisation to develop social projects in empowering people around the highway such as improvement of water and veterinary services and sustainable land use which work well together with conservation.

Many Indian migrants and expatriates have a general tendency to trivialise African culture, practices, and values. However, these initial feelings vanish when you get submerged into today's African reality. Many corporate practices and consumer behaviours move around this which includes a true inner sense of equality and fellow feeling. Gender discrimination is relatively less, and people love to unwind sacrificing aspiration a bit. Many successful Indians make attempts to involve and understand the African way of life. Unless you are friendly with them and appreciate their culture and values, you will not understand their need and expectation. So far, most Indian FMCG companies just export or try to sell same Indian products without any diversification, but sooner or later, this will be challenged. Only a brand extension without feeling the African mind will be a futile strategy very soon. In East and South Africa, large number of Indians are living for generations. Slowly but surely, these two communities are coming closer to each other especially in the last twenty years. I was surprised to see a little African girl speaking Bengali in one of the family ceremonies in my friend's place. After enquiring, I was introduced to a doctor couple who adopted the girl. I also enjoyed a lot when I was invited in a kid's party and a friend's daughter taught me along with her local friends about various ethnic hairstyles. They informed me that most of the styles such as Zulu knots or dreadlocks are traditional ones, but they are flexible and you can bring up new variations easily. These kids were quite informed about Bollywood movies and stars and described to me how African hairstyles can be imbibed into Indian styles (quite amused seeing the agility of them). This cultural integration keeps us ahead of Chinese who have come up in a big way in all parts of Africa. India needs to nurture this route to remain close to the African mind and, thereby, be able to position our goods and services. This is important to note that many Africans are quite conversant with India, but the reverse is not true. We require more and more streamlining of Africa in Indian soil, which I believe is not so easy. Close people-to-people contact, continuous discussion and presentation of modern Africa in India, stories of successful Indian companies, promoting African tourism, cultural shows, etc. are some of the initial things which the government must take up at the earliest.

Cultural linkages are sensitive, and we are required energise it with positive spirits. A slight negative fallback can have huge backlash. Pharmaceutical exports from India have become victims of this. Sometime back, few countries have raised the concern about the spurious drugs exported from India. Many a time, trade agents procure pharmaceutical products from SMEs, and they make attempts to export without having knowledge that many African countries have stricter regulatory environment. Suppose some of these drugs slip into the market crossing the barrier (maybe due to local corruption) and then the news breaks, India will be identified for corrupt practices. This information generally spreads like fire. One African diplomat told me that the government of India must take up steps as Africa needs affordable medicine from India and we need to improve people's confidence. Since 2011, the government of India has introduced mandatory surveillance systems for export of pharmaceutical products from India. It was also found by the Nigerian government that goods produced in other countries carried the label of 'Made in India'. However, when people's trust goes down, it takes a long time to rebuild it. Only changing the policy and more vigilance has partial impact. It is the bond between India and African countries that can act as a catalyst to improve the relationship, and we need to invest on it for continuous positive spillover.

Consumers in African countries are, in general, constrained with fragmented supply chain and a number of corrupt practices at the port along with high non-tariff barriers. As a result, general inflation is always high. Along with this ill-developed financial market cannot ease the production process, and the local industry suffers a lot to finance new projects. Hence, though per capita income in some African countries are growing, high inflation and not availability of easy credit are two major macroeconomic issues which is hindering the growth of middle class. In some countries, borrowing rates are very high (30 per cent average), making it almost impossible to arrange credit from the local market. I have enquired to some Indian companies in West Africa, and all of them are quite vocal about this. More Indian banks must reach there and assist Indian companies in this regard. In general, India must advise these countries about financial market reform and share its own experience to convince.

There are also substantial non-tariff barriers like not-so-easy customs and administrative documentation procedures, complicated inspection requirements, varying, cumbersome and costly transiting procedures which hinder the growth of exports from any country to these countries. Though some regulatory structures are required, many of them are redundant too. Business councils from India and the government must go for more training and awareness programmes before engaging into negotiation. Africa badly requires a better trade facilitation mechanism, and any cooperation strategy from India must include it. Hence, to ensure economic security in the future, India does not only need investment in specific sectors in Africa but also in specific areas of skill development and in enabling business environment. The rise of African middle class and skilled workers in the future will be both an advantage and a challenge for India.

10

Ukraine: What Is There at the End?

Part I

From: Biswajit Nag <biswajit.nag@gmail.com>
Date: Thu, 20 Feb. 2014 at 4.23 p.m.
Subject: From the Heart of Revolution

Yesterday, I received a mail from Vineet with the riot pictures in Kiev. By that time, I read several materials on this, observed closely BBC and CNN, and talked to embassy officials and locals (including professors, students, and people on the street, who could speak English).

Finally, decided to walk down to the epicentre to experience this unique phenomenon. The Independence Square is under control since last several months. Very interestingly, it is popularly called Maidan (also having a Maidan Metro Station as in Kolkata). It is a typical city square where people were in peaceful protest against corruption in general and wanted the current government to go.

I could never imagine that trade agreement issues can be linked with corruption and governance issues and finally can lead to a complete collapse. This entire incident is so deep-rooted and pervasive that my ideas on globalisation are bound to change.

Ukraine is mentally divided into two parts: east wants to remain close to Russia as people have large business stakes and family ties. People can cross borders without visa (I was told), and many of them still appreciate the socialist structure. I experienced the same in Kharkiv. It has Europe's biggest square (world's second after Tiananmen). In the middle of the square, Lenin's statue is still surviving. On the other hand, the western part of the country loves to remain close to Europe.

Both Russia and EU have offered juicy fruits to them. Ukraine has the same crisis as India: low GDP growth, high inflation, high current account deficit, and falling currency. It has received offers to join the Customs Union of RBK (Russia, Belarus, and Kazakhstan) or to join EU. At the initial stage, it has started negotiating a deep comprehensive FTA (DCFTA) with EU. I have read the summary of the agreement. It is really very deep, almost a membership with EU. However, suddenly government backtracked, considering serious implications such as in agriculture, pharmaceutical products, etc. It was on the verge of signing, and the sudden backtracking has created anger among young people who strongly believe that close association with EU will improve institutions, transparency, and reduce the corruption driven by local oligarch. On the other hand, Ukraine's 30-35 per cent of trade is still with Russia. Production networks are with Russian industries. What will happen to those industries if it goes with EU? EU membership and RBK Customs Union are mutually exclusive as all economists know. Hence, the country is in a tug of war between powers and trade agreements. It must be good food for thought for those ardent believers of globalisation.

Kiev city is peaceful, and all demonstrations are localised. But since yesterday, some disturbances are reported from other cities, especially in Lviv. The entire character of protest is very different from ours. In the case of India, everything becomes violent within a moment, and in this case, it is not. Offices, academic institutions, and markets are open; no police is visible except in some strategic location. Last Sunday protesters were going home after having a deal. They wanted the president to resign, which he summarily declined. Instead some discussion was there to change the constitution which the president also failed to do on Monday. That flared up the situation. More surprising, now protesters have started using arms. Russia and EU got engaged in blaming each other, and the situation worsened.

I started walking from the centre using the back side of St Sophia and reached the plaza in front of it. From there straight I could see St Michael. This Orthodox Church offered its space as shelter to protesters. It is now some kind of hospital treating the injured. I could see flags of other countries there supporting the protesters. Most reporters were around this place. The epicentre was just 100 metres away, connecting a small street from the church. I gathered courage to move to that direction a bit and returned swiftly. Life in this part was calm but tensed. Some protesters were carrying tyres to burn in the night. Quite surprisingly, when you turn your face to the other side, you could see a normal life. Ladies were going back home from the office in the evening. So life goes on along with the revolution, which has suddenly turned bloody. To an Indian who has experienced disturbances during the Mandal Commission, demolition of Babri Masjid, after the assassination of Indira Gandhi and Rajiv Gandhi, this is in a true sense a big eye-opener.

While walking down, keeping St Michael at the back, I found a big Soviet building as Ukraine's Foreign Affairs Ministry just a stone's throw distance from the office of the biggest oligarch Akhmetov. It is unimaginable in our country—the existence of a big private company's office so close to the ministry building. The small street was full of urban street sculptures for which Kiev is very famous. These give a pleasant feeling while you are walking on the streets. Protesters were passing by, police were chatting, kids were playing, and old people were enjoying the afternoon sun of February. I was going down using St Andrews Spusk (descent of St Andrews). Protesters have not vandalised any sculpture, or they would have created problems for others. They were there for a cause, not for nuisance, except in last two days when the real fight started. I am really appalled and amazed at the same time seeing the contradiction. Within few hundred metres you could see bloody revolution and beautiful urban arts being appreciated by tourists and local people.

Hope, by the time I reach Delhi, some truce will be there between the two groups which may be a short-term patch. This is a battle between two big powers for their own backyard. It is hard to predict in which direction things will turn. But more difficult is to resolve the mental battle between traditional communist values and exciting capitalistic lifestyle for which citizens are debating for more than twenty years.

During my lectures, in all places (Odessa, Kharkiv, and Kiev), I was asked to explain this sensitive event by students and professors. I could not go into the deep-rooted political issues in which Russia and EU have been involved for some time. Rather I tried to develop an economic explanation and a possible a way out which the country needs to follow at least for next five to ten years. It is clear in the last twenty years, economic decline has been substantial. One professor shared that during Soviet regime, they were financially better off but did not have things to buy due to lack of market orientation under communist rule. Now, people can see and find lots of things around (in shopping malls), but they don't have money to buy. Gas, water, and electricity were subsidised, and these have been gradually lifted. I could imagine the condition of people without heating during this cold weather (today's temperature is –1 to –2 degrees). Ukraine needs to invest substantially in R & D (for which it has a solid base) for manufacturing and also requires to develop brands internationally. Somebody told me when Ukraine would be able to sell its beautiful chocolates in France and Switzerland, we would surely know that country is progressing economically. India imports large amounts of sunflower seeds and oil from Ukraine, but we hardly know it. By the time you are reading this article, you must know that your kitchen is perhaps using Ukrainian sunflower oil to make your food more tasty. However, Ukraine could not develop world-class brands in edible oil. I have seen trains and buses all made during the Soviet time. No progress in automobile and railway industries is visible in the last twenty years. The country has very strong metal sector which can support these industries. It can also build closer relationships with India and China, which can help them to develop low-cost consumer goods industries. Developing international production networks with countries other than EU and Russia are essential, which can reduce the tension and increase the stability. The county still thinks like Soviet but wants to act like EU. These two things cannot go together. I feel this inner contradiction along with the policy paralysis created by oligarchs for their own benefit is the main reasons behind the current conflict.

I am now back at the hotel. Tyres are still burning; I can see the black smoke from my window. I need to pick up a few things from the department stores nearby before the night falls. Walking down to the nearest mall is really a pleasant experience as I need to cross a park. Lovely kids are playing, running, and enjoying amidst of a silence (only the sound of passing cars). Hope this country will be able to build a strong future for these kids who hardly understand the turmoil their nation is passing through.

From: Biswajit Nag <biswajit.nag@gmail.com>
Date: Sat, 22 Feb. 2014 at 3.34 p.m.
Subject: From the Heart of Revolution II

The last part of the writing I could not mail as Internet connectivity was poor at the airport. I saved the draft version and now you can read it.

I have now got my early return ticket as classes have been cancelled in the university due to poor attendance. General panic has broken into the city, and it is difficult to understand which way the things will turn. European ministers are in the city today for negotiations, but protesters are reluctant to believe the president any more.

For the first time, I found that roads in Kiev were empty. The TV news was showing a long queue at the Boryspil Airport; hence, I decided to check out from the hotel quite early. On the way, I stopped at Metro Hypermarket to have some snacks with me as I was getting prepared for the uncertainty. The silence inside the market was noteworthy. There was a long queue. Everyone wanted to have at least a month's stock. Local TV channels were discussing about possible food shortage. I already knew about bread and salt. After sometime, prices might go up exponentially. The astonishing silence reminded me about possible violence in India at the shops during riots. I got to know that some people were collecting food and other essentials for those standing at the Maidan, beating the cold winter nights. As they were not able to join, they took up the role of supplying from the back. I saw dozens of vans full of bread, water bottles, etc. standing just outside the epicentre. My local friend and driver were continuously receiving phone calls from their relatives, and they were busy in explaining that they were safe. Messages have started coming in the mobile phone that if a state of emergency would get declared, all services would be shut down; hence, you must complete your urgent talk at the earliest.

I was stupefied to see this sudden development within hours. The Mercedes car has picked up speed above a hundred so that I can reach the airport fast. The foggy winter evening is making everything hazy, even my thinking. The flashlight from the cars coming from the opposite side is bringing me back to reality.

My friend is now speaking only in Ukranian. The two languages, Ukranian and Russian, are almost two dialects of the same language. Ukraine is a mixed society; Russian, Kazakhs, Polish, Slavics made the country a rich melting pot of variety of cultures. The art and culture promoted by Eastern Orthodox churches along with liberal thinkers, scientists, and great authors made the land a powerful place for progressive thinking. As such Russians are looked as friends, but Russia as a country is thought to have hands in gloves with local oligarchs. Most of the economic institutions and practices are still archaic. Banking rules, taxation, property ownership, and rental practices always invite corruption. People are tired of the situation, and they want a change. Simple tasks become quite complicated. I went to cancel a railway ticket at the central station of Kiev. There are only three specific counters where you can cancel tickets out of fifty reservation counters. After waiting for fifteen to twenty minutes, I received the reply. As the ticket was bought through travel agency, it can't be cancelled by me. After some argument, one gentleman came to the window and agreed to issue me a certificate of cancellation which was supposed to be given to the agent, and in turn, he would receive the money.

We have reached the airport, and surprisingly there was not much queue. I got some time to write down this experience. TV channels were showing piles of dead bodies in a hotel lobby which has been captured by protesters. One doctor was giving her interpretation that snipers were used to kill the protesters as bullets hit mostly heads, necks, and chests. Police in this country mostly use rubber bullets. Gunfires are rare. The patience of police is huge who are there with the protesters since the last three months. In the case of India, police fires at the drop of a hat. This restraint is something to observe. Protesters never imagined that suddenly police would turn violent as explained by the doctor. Alternative theories are also in place. Some outsiders might have come to the epicentre and provoked police. Whatever be the truth, things were going out of hand. If in the next few days the president leaves/resigns, there will be total chaos. The history of Ukraine, in many centuries, repeated similar events as it remained a fertile ground for tug of war between stronger powers. The same is the eventuality even now. Ukraine, as it means, will remain 'on the edge' and perhaps will take a long time to come up as current political and economic problems have spread their wings in many direction. The president will definitely try to negotiate a short run deal by the time I reach Delhi, but its credibility will always be a question.

Part II

Since February, lots of water was flown by Dnieper River. President Viktor Yanukovych demitted his office the day after I left Ukraine. Current president Petro Poroshenko is the fifth elected president of Ukraine. A seasoned politician and a successful businessman (owns large confectionary businesses and a popular TV channel), Poroshenko was an active supporter of the Euro-Maidan protest. On 27 June 2014, Ukraine signed the historic Association Agreements with the EU along with Moldova and Georgia. The euphoria was in the air, but large numbers of people also saw it with scepticism. This agreement is expected to deepen political and economic ties with the EU. As the EU has expanded, these countries have become closer neighbours, and their security, stability, and prosperity increasingly affect the EU's. Closer cooperation between the EU and Ukraine is very important for the EU's external relations. The agreement also includes a Deep and Comprehensive Free Trade Area (DCFTA) which is expected to bring many economic benefits to Ukraine by offering businesses access to the EU's single market. Apart from this success, domestic challenges for the new Ukrainian government is continuing and rising with more complexity. Annexation of Crimea and conflicts in eastern states especially in Donetsk and Luhansk are endlessly haunting the current government, and its relation with rebels and Russia have reached an all-time low. The situation became more volatile and attracted the attention of the world following the crash of the MH17 passenger aircraft.

Let us now concentrate on the gas issue which is surely making the problem more complicated. In case it is not resolved, people in large parts of Europe and especially in Ukraine will face severe cold during the coming winter.

Figure 7: Illustrative Gas Pipeline from Russia to Europe

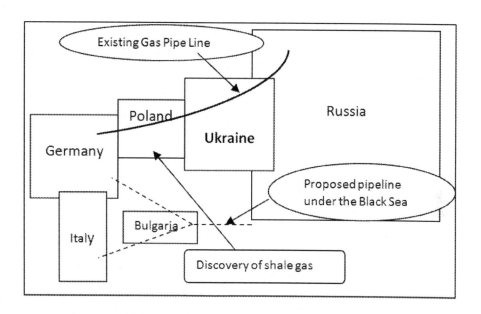

In early June, Russia decided not to supply gas to Ukraine on credit. On the surface, the dispute was about a large unpaid bill, nearly $4.5 billion in total, that Ukraine owed to Gazprom (Russian gas company). The company, 50.01 per cent owned by the Russian state, had asked Ukraine's state gas firm Naftogaz to pay $1.95 billion of the $4.5 billion debt. It said it would continue to supply gas to Europe but raised concern about supplying gas through existing pipelines through Ukraine. Ukraine's existing stock will last till December. EU and USA have requested both Russia and Ukraine to come to a reasonable solution. Ukraine paid partly but was unable to move forward as Russia increased the gas price substantially. Ukraine's gas bill was $268 per 1,000 cubic metres until April 2014. The price has increased to $485.50 thereafter. Ukraine had earlier said it was ready to make the $1.95 billion payment if Russia cut its price to $326. But Russia said $385 was the final offer. This tug of war has reduced the supply of gas from Russia to Europe also. Currently, gas is supplied following a strict requirement schedule of Europe. About a fifth of the European Union's supply of natural gas flows through Ukraine. Ukraine itself imported from Russia 63 per cent of the natural gas it consumed in 2012, producing the remaining 37 per cent domestically. The current cut-off had a serious impact on countries like Bulgaria, Greece, Macedonia, Romania, Croatia, and Turkey all reported a halt in gas shipments from Russia through Ukraine. Croatia has even reduced the supply to industrial customers.

There are two more important issues connected to gas supply. Few years back, a proposal was mooted to develop a new South Stream pipeline below the Black Sea from Russia to European borders. Several European countries agreed to the proposal. However, recently, EU has raised a concern that this pipeline may conflict with European competition laws regarding open access as Russian firms will have dominating effect. In April 2014, during the middle of the conflict in Ukraine, the European Parliament adopted a non-binding resolution opposing the South Stream gas pipeline and recommending a search for alternative sources of gas supplies for the EU. This has created a new confusion as some parts of the project are scheduled to start soon especially in Austria and Bulgaria. Russia has filed a complaint at WTO against EU stating that it has violated international norms of gas transit facilities and current law is forcing Gazprom to allow other gas producers to use this dedicated pipeline. So at one side, Ukraine owes huge amounts to a Russian company, and secondly, Russia's prized project of South Stream is under question and, hence, their future domination in European gas market is doubtful. Another issue of shale gas discovery in Poland has posed a new challenge and made the future gas market situation quite tricky. Poland is experiencing the largest exploration boom in Europe, and if Polish reserves turn out to be even half as big as expected, the country could quickly turn into a net exporter of natural gas. Ukraine, being a bordering country, has high potentiality too. Many US and EU exploration firms are now eyeing on Ukraine for exploration. If a sufficient amount of gas is discovered in Poland and partly in Ukraine, Gazprom's dominance in these markets will not remain. The current gas conflict is no more limited to Ukraine and Russia. Rather it has wide wings, and many other European countries have their own interest.

Amidst of this crisis, India will remain confused and a mute spectator because of its historical good relations with all of them: Ukraine, Russia, and EU. During my lectures in universities and interactions with the faculty community in Ukraine, one thing has come up clearly. Ukraine requires to learn modern business practices and increase its managerial efficiency. So far, it has focused on technology, natural resources, and capacity in making capital goods and machinery. The nature of competition in these areas is different from consumer goods and services. As the global economy is becoming more service-oriented, even in the manufacturing sector, service components become critical in enhancing competitiveness. These include modern banking and insurance services, accounting services, professional services, etc. The weakness of Ukraine in these areas is clear, and people expect that India can contribute. Most of the industries' supply chain is still extended to Russia, and current conflict has a major impact on the industrial production also. More than 30 per cent of its trade is still with Russia, and in the past, Ukraine hardly looked towards East for developing industrial collaboration. Current conflict has pushed intellectuals to think in terms of closer relationships with China and India to diffuse the future risk and look for more cost-effective solutions in the consumer goods segments and services and also for possible technology collaboration.

Since the collapse of USSR, Ukraine has become one of India's major allies in the region. India was one of the first countries to recognize the independence of Ukraine in December 1991, and in March 1992 Ukraine's first president made his maiden foreign visit and that to India. Over the years, these two countries have developed a number of treaties and collaboration in defence, scientific endeavours, and trade and economic issues. Since President Kalam's visit to Kiev in 2005, the idea of cooperation in more specific areas such as pharmaceutical, biotechnology, information technology, higher education, etc. are being pursued. A proposal of comprehensive partnership between India and Ukraine was declared during the visit by Ukrainian president Yanukovych to New Delhi in December 2012. Despite such a close relationship, the general feeling is that both countries can do much more than what has been achieved so far. A common view is that Ukraine is now more tilted towards European Union for their immediate growth objective, and India has also not explored Ukraine sufficiently due to a host of reasons such as language barrier, lack of cultural linkage, higher risk of investment, and political instability. Indian cultures are more popular in Ukraine as local people in big cities participate in Indian festivals such as Holi, Diwali, etc. Indian dance and Hindi language are increasingly becoming part of the academic curriculum, and many people pursue them for their career. But the reverse is not true. The knowledge of Ukraine in India is extremely limited outside the top few big cities. I visited a few big libraries in Kiev and Kharkiv and got zapped by seeing the Indology section. Since the nineteenth century, scholars have studied history, literature, and religion of India. Translation of modern Indian books into Russian and Ukrainian language is also not uncommon. Comparisons between Tagore and Shevchenko seem to be a common starting point of discussion for most of the people who are interested in India. On 25 January 2014, Odessa Central Library celebrated the 190th birth anniversary of great Bengali poet Madhusudan Dutta. On the contrary, the culture, history, and literature of Ukraine are still not popular in India. Perhaps, Ukraine needs to promote these more vigorously in India.

The trade relation between India and Ukraine is very skewed. India's import (excluding defence goods) has been approximately US$2.6 billion in 2013, and its export was close to US$500 million only. In 2000, India was mostly importing iron and steel and related products, but in 2011, close to 50 per cent of the total import has been sunflower oil and related products. India imports more than US$1 billion edible oil, and it is experiencing a significant growth. Globally, Ukraine could not brand their product because of lack of marketing skill, knowledge related to trade rules including WTO issues, and food processing technology. As a result, in a common Indian household, we hardly know that our kitchen is using sunflower oil from Ukraine with high probability. Other important products India imports from Ukraine are fertiliser, mineral oil, metal products, chemical products, etc. On the other hand, India's export basket mostly consists of pharmaceutical products (close to 30 per cent of our exports to Ukraine in 2012), electrical products and accessories (13 per cent), automobile and components (9 per cent), plastic, chemicals, tobacco, tea, spices, textile, etc. Several Indian companies have also invested in Ukraine, but it is far less than Indian ventures in other countries. Companies such as Ranbaxy, Dr Reddy's, Cadila, Tata International, etc. are actively engaged in business with Ukraine. In 2001, the amount of the Indian direct investment to the Ukrainian economics was about US$ 1.8 million, and twenty-nine enterprises with Indian investment were registered. Indian investment was expected to rise after the visit of President Yanukovych to India in 2012. It was expected that Indian investment would rise to US$5–7 billion, but it did not realise due to the events which spurt up during the end of 2013 and the beginning of 2014. Also several Indian pharmaceutical companies have the apprehension that Western pharmaceutical companies will mount pressure on Ukrainian authorities both to reduce import from India and close down the production of Indian assisted companies in Ukraine. Already due to current crisis, local currency Hryvnia has got depreciated against US dollar, implying India's loss in comparative advantage.

India has a number of scientific collaborations with Ukraine. Joint scientific and technical fairs are held in the past. Exchange of faculty and researchers between the two countries are now a regular affair. Since India's independence, the country has been benefitted from Ukrainian technological skill under the Soviet banner. Steel plant at Bhilai was set up with the technical assistance from Ukraine. For many years in the power generation sector, Ukraine's contribution in India has been noteworthy. In the defence area, Ukraine's steel sheets have been used in Indian warships; it has been a supplier of tanks and other major equipment. Ukraine also maintains India's air force aircrafts and modernise them. Ukrainian public joint stock company Kyivmetrobud [22] are engaged in building railway tunnels in Jammu and Kashmir, where underground builders share experience of tunnel building in surface rocks. Ukraine has a rich experience in deep tunnel building. Kiev metro has some of the deepest stations in the world. The Arsenalna station is the deepest metro station in the world, at 107 metres deep, and the Universytet station has one of the longest escalators (eighty-seven metres long). Many stations have two long and intimidating escalators in a row. I asked about the reasons behind such deep tunnels. The answer was obvious. It was the safe passage during the possible bomb attacks especially in the time of the cold war. It is noteworthy that all such mighty companies are mainly public companies. Ukraine has made some efforts to privatise some of them, but sheer lack of experience pushed these companies to losses with few exceptions. In case of medical education, Ukraine has occupied its own position. During the Soviet era, big hospitals were made and subsidised, and cheap medical education was promoted. Even today, universities and medical colleges receive large grants from the government. Currently in Ukraine, there are about 4,000 Indian students. The most popular qualifications remain medical and technical professions, mainly due to the high quality of their teaching at a moderate training cost. Several Indian doctors and engineers have decided to stay back after their formal education. Hence, India will be deeply influenced by the current crisis in Ukraine. Politically and economically, we are linked, and this cannot be ignored.

Figure 8: India's Trade with Ukraine

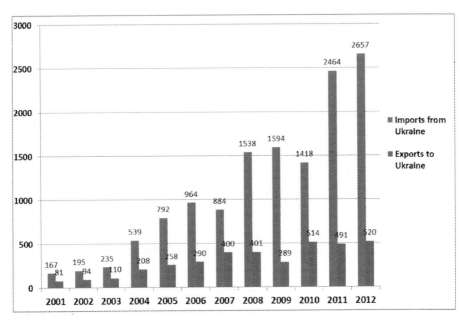

Calculated from Trademap (Trade Map, International Trade Centre, www.intracen.org/marketanalysis)

Myself and Vadim got down at Arsenalna station and started walking down towards the Park of Glory. The sun was about to set, roads were busy, people were enjoying street food, and elderly citizens were relaxing inside the park. It was cold and windy. I was appreciative of mighty structures and technological marvels Kiev city has offered. These days, many people think those structures as ugly Soviet-style buildings. Still the landscape around the park, buildings, and Pechersk Hills on the Dnieper River in the evening was giving a sense of past glory. We stood for a while in front of the candle like Famine Memorial. This was built in memory of thousands of people who died during the series of famines in 1920s and especially during 1932–1933. People strongly believe that was a man-made famine and equivalent to genocide which was done on behest of the Soviet power to control Ukraine. It was then dark, slowly and silently we were going out of the garden. Snow patches and slippery pathways were taking us to Pechersk Lavra monastery. The church bell was ringing. The sounds of hymns were everywhere. The elaborate practice in Eastern Orthodox Church in a moment took us 1,000 years back. During Soviet time, religious practices went back behind the curtain. Today's non-communist Ukraine has brought back the tradition. Byzantine artworks and frescos on the wall in dimmed candle lights became alive. They were the witness of this place which faced many attacks in the last 1,000 years, even during the last world war. Ukraine's Patriotic War Museum was close by. We started walking down the slippery road. It was dark and eerie. The other side of the city was burning for freedom and came together to fight against corruption, and here, under the dark roads, the communist-style bold stonework were telling us the stories of war heroism. Illuminated by spotlights, the figures with guns, flags, sickle, and hammer literally had an imposing impression. Then we finally arrived at the great statue of *The Motherland* overlooking the river. Time stopped for a while. My mind was dwindling between the Soviet time, today's free Ukraine, and also the uncertain future. I came back to the reality with the SMS tone in my mobile phone which carries a 'keep safe' message from a well-wisher.

My phone said it's 8.30 p.m. Suddenly, I felt the cold and started walking fast. We had to walk at least a few kilometres to reach the nearest metro station. We were walking down, keeping the history behind, and towards the more populated area. On the way, I got to know a number of stories on the Chernobyl disaster. Even today, Kiev's weather forecast provides the radiation level along with other parameters. Currently, radiation in Kiev is much lower than the minimum danger level. Vadim described that he had to flee from the city after the incident and did his schooling in Moscow.

It was a fairly crowded train. No one would realise the tension the country was facing. I was watching the faces one by one but did not see any worry. My tired body could not sustain, and I fell asleep. Suddenly, I woke up with a sweet melody; a little girl was walking with her mother inside the train, singing a song and asking for help. We reached Olimpiska station. A large office crowd got down. I tried to locate the little child, but she vanished in the crowd with her uncertain future in hand. The melody was still there in mind, and I was feeling melancholic. Soon, we reached Palats Ukraina, our destination.

My heart was heavy but my mind was agile to seek more information about the general problem of CIS countries in post-Soviet era. Many of them have not done enough during the transition period. Newly born CIS countries became prized possessions of many earlier powerful individuals from the Soviet period. They had deep influence in the politics, changed rules for their own benefits, halted transparency, and forced consumers to live a difficult life with less availability of public services and no benefits of free market economy. As a result, modern institutions did not develop, and today they are unable to cope with the force of globalisation. On the other hand, a ticket to EU will not solve these issues overnight. Sound macroeconomic management, handling international risk, improving comparative advantage of their products, capitalising on their skill especially in technology, etc. are the tasks in hand. These are also not easy things. In May 2014, the government of Ukraine has brought out a consensus forecast with the assistance from UNDP. It has identified a number of foreign and domestic risks (see the tables below) which is going to influence Ukraine's uncertain future. With international mediation, political problems may subside sooner or later, but economic problems will remain and might push Ukraine to the fringe.

Foreign Risks
Escalation of Ukrainian–Russian conflict
Breaking trade and economic relations with Russian Federation
Curtailing of investment plans by foreign companies or postponement of their realization terms for future period
Recession of the economy of Russian Federation through imposing sanctions by countries of the world
Further complication of foreign economic relations with members of Customs Union
Reducing the inflow of foreign investment and massive outflow of capital from Ukraine due to the political instability
Deficit of external funding and shrinkage of possibilities of access to the international capital markets
Slow recovery of the global economy
Increase in the cost of external borrowing for Ukrainian corporations
Signing the economic part of agreement about free trade zone with EU
Deterioration of external economic conjuncture: strengthening volatility of prices at the world raw materials markets
Decrease of prices at the world energy markets
Failure to obtain planned financing from the IMF

Increase of process at the world energy markets
Further introduction of other countries allowed by the WTO trade restrictions that adversely affect the Ukrainian export
Increasing the debt crisis in euro area
Slow growth of the USA economy
Strengthening of the military conflict in the Middle East
Euro devaluation and decrease of demand in the European Union

Source: Ukraine: Development Prospects Consensus Forecast (2014); Ministry of Economic Development and Trade of Ukraine

Domestic Risks
Substantial increase of natural gas prices for municipal heat and power engineering enterprises
Remaining low-credit activity of commercial banks
Accumulation of the population's negative inflation expectations
Substantial increase of natural gas tariffs for the population
Substantial increase of natural gas tariffs for industry
Expansion of the real economy's insolvency
Risks of destabilization in the banking sector
Strengthening of devaluation tendencies at the monetary market
Deterioration at the labour market: reducing the number of employees and increasing the number of unemployed
Significant growth in the state budget deficit and cash gaps of the pension fund, other state social insurance funds, and Naftohaz Ukrainy NJSC
Accumulation of VAT refund debt
The effectiveness of the implementation of the new policy of the government of Ukraine
Carrying out considerable emission to finance the budget deficit
Increase of debt on payment for housing and public utilities
The growth of wage arrears
Receiving high yield of crops
Default on obligations
Privatization of state property at a cost lower than the potential due to the need to obtain primary financial resources to financing state obligations

Increase of revaluation tendencies at the monetary market
Abandonment by the National Bank of Ukraine from flexible exchange rate policy
Restoration of state sovereignty of Ukraine in Crimea
Decline of the population's inflation expectations

Source: Ukraine: Development Prospects Consensus Forecast (2014); Ministry of Economic Development and Trade of Ukraine

Conclusion:

Globalisation and Tools for Analysis

I was angry with my friend:
I told my wrath, my wrath did end.
I was angry with my foe:
I told it not, my wrath did grow.

William Blake

lobalisation has brought both excitement and frustration. During the heydays, people were arguing that openness and freedom would change the future of a country. It did not work in that way, and now critics put forward the logic that reckless globalisation and uncontrolled finance capital have pushed the globe to the edge. The conflict between modernism and postmodernism are here to stay for long, implying the coexistence of logical yet diffused and complex structure of arguments. The constant tug of war between various arguments of how to make our world a better place has taken the dominant position. The arguments are not only to find right or wrong, true or false, black or white but also to analyse the shades of grey spots between black and white. The logic to explain global phenomena is substantially driven by our perceptions based on our own experience and scientific analysis of information available. It is difficult to develop our views in a linear fashion due to the constant source of new information. Hence, we require a structure to analyse them based on history, culture, tradition, political situation, economic condition, etc. There are plenty of organisations who provide country analysis in terms of commentary on macroeconomic situations, political conditions, forecasting of various growth parameters, etc. People and companies develop their views based on these information. In many cases, these information can lead us to wrong direction also. For example, the information about the size of Indian middle class consisting of 400 million people offering a huge market can be quite misleading as anybody who is above the poverty line can potentially be in the middle-class bracket unless definition of middle class and their purchasing capacity is clearly spelt out. The ability to intermix quantitative and qualitative information and dexterity to balance between two opposite views are the main proficiency we need to absorb. The book has juxtaposed many conflicting situations and contradiction in public policies to portray the arguments from both sides. Our world has become more vulnerable and prone to economic crisis, environmental disasters, and severe political unrest. As a result, it is natural that any argument on international business environment will face counterintuitive logics turning a discourse into powerful polemic.

Globalisation is a process which has a significant implication on the economic, political, and social fabric of nations. It is a contentious process. Ever since the term was first used, scholars have debated its meaning and use. By the end of the twentieth century, the meaning and merits of globalisation were contested in the media and on the streets. Intellectual debate blended with political conflict. The world is currently experiencing an increasing interaction among different countries through the growth in trade, investment, and capital flows. Countries are now interwoven with each other, and that means, economic downturn in USA will lead to job loss in China. Many perceive this interaction as a worldwide drive towards formation of a globalised economic system. This is associated with the fast development in modern communications and information technologies. Nowadays, knowledge and culture can be shared around the world simultaneously. This entire phenomenon has an increasing impact on the society and economy at the local or global level and is popularly known as globalisation.

Many people consider that there is nothing new about globalisation. The spreading of world religions, the huge development of empires in the eighteenth and nineteenth centuries, spreading of European cultures to all the world remind that the idea of globalisation is hardly a new concept. But there have been different historical forms of globalisation, and the contemporary conjuncture is new.[23] The interconnectedness of the societies existed for years. However, the world has never experienced with this intensity and velocity the transformation and integration of societies. The wave of globalisation started with the falling transport costs and more accentuated by the fast reduction of trade barriers. The Internet revolution brought a new dimension of globalisation. Finally, today's globalisation is largely directed by the global institutions: World Trade Organisations (WTO), World Bank, International Monetary Fund (IMF), and United Nations (UN) which was not the case in the eighteenth or nineteenth century.

For the economist, globalisation is essentially the emergence of a global market. For the historian, it is an epoch dominated by global capitalism. A sociologist interprets globalisation as the convergence of social preferences in matters of lifestyle and social values. A political scientist is concerned about the gradual erosion of state sovereignty due to a wave of globalisation. While all discipline-specific studies of globalisation do advance a rich and nuanced understanding, each discipline merely explains a part of the phenomenon. From a multidisciplinary angle, globalisation may be treated as a phenomenon, a philosophy, and a process which affects the human kind profoundly as any other event ever did before (Khan, 2003).[24] For the international business, globalisation has put forward a new challenge juxtaposing apparently contradicting factors. For example, at one side there is an effort to position standardized products globally (such as electronic goods from Apple), on the other hand companies are addressing the heterogeneities among the society offering diversified product basket (such as in automobiles). The challenge for new-age managers is to accommodate culture, rituals, and norms of different societies while selling products internationally, bringing the issue of global division of labour through international production networks (IPNs). In an era of globalisation, a company may procure raw materials from any part of the world; it may divide its production process into various sub-processes (located in more than one country) and finally can sell it in different countries. Hence, the challenge is to handle international supply chain and distribution channel of a product or even a service. With the effort from global organisations, many policies around the world have streamlined, but effectiveness of policies and country priorities are largely dependent on economic vulnerability of the country, state of existing institutions, governance style and traditions, etc.

which are widely different. Hence, through WTO negotiation, several trade policies issues have been addressed, but the complications in international supply chain have not come down substantially.

Arguments on globalisation are clearly divided. Optimists look forward to a global village, linked together by the Internet, and benefiting from ever-increasing material well-being through the expansion of trade and flow of investment. Pessimists see a frightful corporate tyranny destroying the environment and sweeping away all that is healthy and meaningful to human existence. In other words, globalisation creates new markets and wealth, even as it causes widespread suffering, disorder, and unrest. It is both a source of repression and a catalyst for global movements of social justice and emancipation. So at the one hand, countries are joining hands for free trade agreements and multinational companies are invited with tax holidays. On the other hand, global groups are organizing themselves for environmental standards, labour standards, and basic human rights.[25] Today's managers and policymakers need to absorb this incongruity while making their strategy and addressing development as well as corporate challenge.

The book starts with culture, perception, and softer issues. The main points portrayed in this section are the importance to appreciate different cultures and ability to read the finer points to develop our own perception and communicate it. The power of communication in influencing others to interpret any incident or to promote any product or services is unchallenged. The art is to develop new dimension from the existing information and capacity to cultivate a vision (a la selling a balloon under Eiffel Tower). Why does the same product or same strategy not work in different countries? There are a number of explanations available in the Internet but most of them are general. You require specific information around the issues you are concerned with. Government officials require a different skill while dealing with Chinese or American officials. Same is true for corporate managers. The softer issues around tradition, food habits, priorities towards emerging fashion and music could be influencing tools while negotiating hard for business or economic issues with citizens from a foreign country. Your ability to bring out the specific information through the communication skill with due sensitivity to others' priority is the key to success. A brilliant product sometimes get diffused if it does not match with perception and priorities of the target audience (refer to the difference between Joshua Bell playing violin in New

York Metro in a busy morning versus Jean-Pierre Lignian playing cello on a Sunday morning at Montmartre, Paris, in a relaxed environment). Similarly, to understand the mind of people from other countries, we require to recognise their priorities, such as issues related to fashion and design for Italians or family values for Indians or hygiene for Thai people. These delicate apparently non-economic issues have huge importance in marketing and promotion. For example, we can mention about the concept of 'family pack' in India or the ever-growing detergent market with new variants in Thailand. Food is also an important tool which acts as catalyst in bridging two cultures, and it is being experimented as contrivance to improve tolerance among competing cultures. Hence, to promote diplomacy and improve corresponding business environment sensitivity towards foreign food culture is extremely important. In the second part, we have focused more on economic and public policy related issues. Interpretation of economic policy, corruption, socio-economic status, and macroeconomic data analysis is at the core of environment analysis. Forces of globalisation lead us to think that all economic problems have a market solution. However, state of institutions and governance structure of many countries in the developing world make us believe that market failures are more than common. Artificial currency crisis or fixed exchange related problems along with lack of prudent financial institutions and shallow credit market are the product of both existing philosophy behind policy regime as well as lack of capacity to develop the right kind of policies. We also require to understand structural problems of many countries. It could be geographical disadvantage or stock of large unskilled population or underdeveloped institutions. Free market economy requires the strong government more to ensure stability. Public utilities and services are increasingly being managed by private players, but success depends on the nature of regulatory environment and control on corruption. More than the knowledge of globalisation, policymakers and managers need to know how to adapt, react, and develop new policy stance to adjust to new global situations. As mentioned in the book, market solution may not always be an optimal strategy to solve a management conflict efficiently especially when losers have the capability to organise countervailing action even internationally. In the last section, some of the country-specific issues have been highlighted. The experience of these countries provides enough learning opportunities. For example, how the Japanese innovation system is integrated with academics and other stakeholders such as civil society, municipality, etc. is an important knowledge which we can infuse in our system partly. Similarly, the novelty in designing research subsidies in an integrated fashion has helped Japan to bring a unique blend of public–private partnership. Under this system, in public-funded projects, the private sector participates and collaborates with universities, research laboratories, and SMEs. The objective of the project is to commercialise the output through developing shrink-wrapped products and to fragmentise the production system. Japan is determined to bring a path-breaking solution in environmental issues linking its capacity in electronics and computing with mechanical engineering through an inclusive strategy connecting all stakeholders. Unlike Japan, open innovation system has proliferated in USA due to the supply of venture capital in the innovation sector. This has a massive spin-off effect in the IT industry especially in developing mobile application, cloud computing, and big data analytics. These experiences must guide our direction to develop our innovation policy. The future of globalisation will lead to competition among nations under a series of major constraints. The depleting non-renewable resources will affect the production system, and this will be coupled with stringent regulation to protect environment and social fabric. Countries and companies need to adhere to higher labour standards and give values to basic human rights. Hence, to improve productivity and to keep buoyancy in the competitive world, the most important prerequisite is the investment in R & D. More collaborative policies and co-opting strategies may work in the medium run. The chapter on Africa highlights India's three eminent economic security issues: food, energy, and natural resources. The continent can provide us all three in case we carefully design our policy in a circular way. More investment in Africa in soft issues including education and health will help us to get skilled, knowledgeable, and healthy workers which in turn make our imports from Africa cheaper. In turn, it can be our market especially in FMCG and capital goods. Rising African middle class with higher spending power can be a major source of India's growth sometime maybe after 2020. Our investment in technology with cheaper energy and resources from Africa can help India to improve its manufacturing competitiveness. Globalisation has also contributed through increased political instability with domestic and international unrest. Managing global production system and protecting the country's interest using economic diplomacy will be another important area where countries like India need to concentrate. The example of Ukraine has been brought in the book to uphold this idea. So far, India's economic loss has not been assessed, but it is clear that our exports and imports have gotten severe shock. India's investment in Ukraine will be in question. In the future, India's military and project-based collaborations will also be affected. Such crisis may break any time in the future in another part of the world as competitive space for developing countries are further getting narrowed. Companies and countries are required to invest resources in developing special negotiating skills to handle economic, political, and environmental crisis. As the global value chain is getting integrated, any such crisis may have serious repercussions on the production system as well as in the life of millions of citizens (such as the Fukushima issue or cutting down of gas supply in Ukraine, etc.).

To analyse any country and its economic and business environment, we require both quantitative and qualitative information. Though there is no definitive way to collect qualitative information, analytical ability requires knowledge of history, culture, contemporary, socio-economic, and political background of the country. On the other hand, a large number of publicly available websites provide quantitative information on countries which range from data on macroeconomic variables to information on socio-economic issues. You require patience, inquisitiveness, and knowledge on statistics/econometrics to decipher the real story out of the huge data available in those sites. To start with, you can develop an approach based on the following table. At the first stage, learn about the modern history, development stories, and consumer profile of the country. Subsequently, read about the contemporary political structure, nature of labour market, judicial system, and overall sense of freedom citizens enjoy in that country. Start the macroeconomic data analysis, identifying basic variables such as GDP, national income, per capita GDP, contribution of agriculture, industry, and services. Analyse other variables such as consumer price index, interest rate, and movement of exchange rate. Plot their trend in MS Excel. Identify the ups and downs. Question yourself about what happened to the country when graphs were going up or coming down. Identify the major policy changes and read about their background. Next, turn towards the external sector. Generally you get large numbers of data to analyse export and import trend. Do an analysis about the export-import basket and identify main trading partners. Identify where your own country stands as a trading partner of the country you are studying. Do the same analysis for investment regime. Now, start reading about the contemporary economic policy the country is pursuing, especially manufacturing policy, trade policy, investment regime, nature of trade and investment barriers, regulatory environment, trade facilitation issues. At this stage, you may like to search for more specific information about the concerned sector which you are looking for. You may search in the database of research articles and decide to write emails to few knowledgeable people, including the commercial wing of your embassy in the foreign country or chambers of commerce. At the last stage, look for issues related to distribution channel, purchase habits, media habits, occasions for consumption, etc. At this level, analysis of information available in Doing Business database and Logistics Performance Index of the World Bank will be very useful. Other qualitative areas such as corruption level and economic freedom can also be studied. Perhaps you require more intimate discussion with local people or those who have lived in that country for long. Here comes your ability to relate the stories with the history, culture, and evolution of the society.

Table 10: Identifying Issues to Analyse Business and Economic Environment of a Country

Stage 1	Stage 2	Stage 3
Learn about the Background: History, development stories, contemporary political structure, nature of labour market, judicial system, and overall sense of freedom citizens enjoy in that country	*Policy Analysis* Start with the country's overall macroeconomic policy. Identify major reform it has carried out recently.	Doing Business data analysis

Logistics Performance Index data analysis

Enabling Trade Index data analysis

Corruption Data analysis |
Macroeconomic Trend Analysis GDP, national income, per capita GDP, contribution of agriculture, industry, and services, consumer price index, interest rate, movement of exchange rate, etc.	*Sectoral Policy Analysis* Trade Policy Regime explaining the nature of tariffs, non-tariffs, and other barriers, trade facilitation issues, etc.	Collect information about the nature of distribution channel, price formation, media habits, consumer profile, consumption pattern either by personal interaction through email or by visit.
Data Analysis for External Sector Identify major trading partners, identify major products that are being traded, do balance of payment analysis.	Investment Policy Regime analysis explaining nature of regulation for foreign investment, intellectual property rights, repatriation of profit issues, technology and innovation policy, etc.	*Do Some Risk Analysis* You may do an advanced data analytics or develop your judgemental view on all information you have collected.
Analyse the nature of trade engagement your country has with the country you are studying. Calculate your country's share in the trade basket of the foreign country.	Manufacturing policy analysis to identify nature of competition, regulation on sourcing, pricing, nature of subsidies and incentives, etc. Government policies towards formation of industrial clusters should also be studied.	Round up your analysis by identifying compulsion, obligation, tradition, and expectation (your views).
Analyse the foreign direct investment inflow.	Study the existing research output.	

Table 11: Some Useful Publicly Available Database for Information on Business and Economic Environment of a Country

Overview of an Economy

CIA World Fact Book https://www.cia.gov/library/publications/the-world-factbook/

EIU Country Analysis (partly subscription based) http://www.eiu.com/home.aspx

World Travel and Tourism Council (Focus on tourism industry but useful) http://www.wttc.org/research/economic-impact-research/country-reports/

WTO Trade Policy Review: http://www.wto.org/english/tratop_e/tpr_e/tp_rep_e.htm#bycountry

USTR Country Reports: http://www.ustr.gov/about-us/trade-toolbox/country-profiles

Economic Indicators and Other Country-Level Data

International Financial Statistics Yearbook of IMF: http://www.imfstatistics.org/imf/

National Accounts Data: http://unstats.un.org/unsd/snaama/SelectionCountry.asp

World Development Indicators:
http://web.worldbank.org/WBSITE/EXTERNAL/DATASTATISTICS/0,,contentMDK:21298138~pagePK:64133150~piPK:64133175~theSitePK:239419,00.html

UN Statistics: http://unstats.un.org/unsd/default.htm

Least Developed Country Reports: http://unctad.org/en/pages/aldc/Least%20Developed%20Countries/The-Least-Developed-Countries-Report.aspx

Trade Statistics and Related Issues

Commodity Trade: http://comtrade.un.org/db/default.aspx

UNCTAD Statistics: http://www.unctad.org/Templates/Page.asp?intItemID=1584

WITS Database: www.wits.worldbank.org

World Investment Report: http://unctad.org/en/pages/DIAE/World%20Investment%20Report/WIR-Series.aspx

World Tariff Profile: http://www.wto.org/english/res_e/reser_e/tariff_profiles_e.htm

Trade in Value-Added Database: http://stats.oecd.org/index.aspx?queryid=47807

Development and Socio-Economic Indicators
Education, Health, Employment, Gender Issues, etc.
Human Development Index: http://hdr.undp.org/en/statistics/
UN Social Indicators: http://unstats.un.org/unsd/demographic/products/socind/
Millennium Development Goals Database: http://mdgs.un.org/unsd/mdg/
Default.aspx
WHO Country Reports: http://www.who.int/countries/en/

Doing Business
Doing Business Indicators: http://www.doingbusiness.org/
or http://data.worldbank.org/indicator/IC.BUS.EASE.XQ
Logistics Performance Indicators: http://lpi.worldbank.org/
Enabling Trade Index: http://www.weforum.org/reports/
global-enabling-trade-report-2014
Global Competitiveness Report: http://www.weforum.org/reports/
global-competitiveness-report-2013-2014
Corruption Perception Index: http://www.transparency.org/research/cpi/overview
Global Innovation Index: http://www.globalinnovationindex.org/content.
aspx?page=GII-Home
Index of Economic Freedom: http://www.heritage.org/index/
Hofstede's Cultural Index: http://geert-hofstede.com/the-hofstede-centre.html

Note: Some of the organisations bring out yearly reports. The URL is connecting to the latest available report. It may change from one year to another.

Afterword

Doubt is not a pleasant state of mind,
but certainty is absurd.

Voltaire

I was quite excited when a group of students enticed me to document the stories and facts shared in the class while teaching the Global Business Environment course or in the sideline of Trade Policy course. My excitement turned into worry while I finished the manuscript. I was anxious whether I would be able to reach the reader with the right kind of message. There were a few questions in my mind.

Why do we need this book?

There are standard textbooks which provide a structured pedagogy with clear learning objectives, definitions, examples, diagrams, summaries, and questions at the end of each chapter. Textbooks now have good supplementary tools such as additional reading materials, PowerPoint presentations, and a collection of multiple choice and essay type questions. Teaching has become smoother but linear. Interdisciplinary approach, which is the main cornerstone of business education, is missing in most of these books. We are required to bring tools from economics, marketing, finance, political science, etc. for a clear understanding of economic and business environment. GDP, consumption pattern, inflation, and for that matter, any economic indicator are just numbers. It reveals little and hides most. Some students are more motivated to interpret statistics and facts and start studying materials from the Internet. Invariably, they move away from the objective-oriented study material to subjective areas of learning. In this world of over-information, these students don't find any direction and mostly end up with confusion. They are unable to develop generalized views from fragmented pieces of information. Textbooks are important as they help us to build the concept in a systematic manner. However, it misses the fun of combining various things together and constructs new perceptions. Many a time, while walking on the street, we tend to link certain events/observations with some of the theories we read somewhere. This book has primarily taken up this approach which gives importance on the free flow of thinking and building up your own opinion. Readers do not need to accept my views, but my writing will be successful if it leads the reader to alternative thinking. The freewheeling out-of-the-box thinking may lead to new arguments providing a new dimension to international business environment analysis. This book cannot be a substitute to a textbook. Rather it can be used as a reference while studying the subject. Most of the textbooks provide developed country views on topics related to culture, development issues, and protectionism in the developing world. However, there exist alternative views which justify the existence of some kind of policy stance. Many technology and policy solutions are emerging from the developing world, which we popularly tag as south-south solutions. Our readers from the developing world will be able to appreciate them as these issues are within their experiential learning paradigm. The interdisciplinary approach will also impart students to ask meaningful questions and find logical answers.

Who is *Rafiki*?

Rafiki represents or symbolizes ideas and concepts related to friendship. Our conscience is our closest friend, and we trust its ability to logically decipher complex global phenomena in its own way. The facts and analysis on globalisation may create a bipolar world, but it's our own analysis based on information, data, and interaction with people that will be of paramount importance. Knowing a country means knowing people and sharing your views, observations, and experiences with others. All of us are now connected through social media. We get news and views not only from popular media but also from our friends and acquaintances, those who are hooked on to Facebook, LinkedIn, and WhatsApp. Everyone is having their own opinion, and people are no more hesitant to share it. This unique phenomenon emanated from the force of information technology and, driven by globalisation, perhaps will provide a new dimension to understanding the dynamics of the world economy in terms of reasoning out the role of history, culture, religion, corruption, politics, etc. in shaping up the world for tomorrow. People are crossing the geography, going to new places, and exploring new cultures since prehistoric times. At the end, all travellers need a friend who becomes their guide and philosopher. They explore the new world through the vision of a common man. I was always amazed to get assistance from unknown people in India and other parts of the world, pushing me to think that people are the same everywhere. It is the context, artificial erection of certain systems, and prejudices that force us to think differently. *Rafiki* is our true friend, a traveller, and a storyteller. It embraces the stories of people's lives, expectations, and agonies.

Index

Endnotes

1   Sen Amartya (1995). 'Our Culture, Their Culture', delivered as Satyajit Ray lecture given at Nandan, Calcutta (22.12.1995) and later published in the book *The Argumentative Indian* (Penguin, 2005).

2   As per June 2011, Doing Business ranking by the World Bank.

3   Marco Fortis: Competitiveness and Export Performance of Italy (Fondazione Edison; Università Cattolica Di Milano): http://www.dt.tesoro.it/export/sites/sitodt/modules/ documenti_en/analisi_progammazione/eventi/Fortis_-_slide.pdf

4   Fortis Marco (2010): Competitiveness and Export Performance of Italy http://www. dt.tesoro.it/export/sites/sitodt/modules/documenti_en/analisi_progammazione/ eventi/Fortis_paper.pdf accessed on 1 December 2013

5   Kaushik Basu (2011). *An Economist's Miscellany* (Oxford) 53–55.

6   Author provided his inputs to the United Nations in similar line in 2009.

7   Ibid.

8   As an example, RFD link for Ministry of Rural Development (2012–2013) is given http://rural.nic.in/sites/downloads/general/RFD_2012_13.pdf. Please refer to section 2 which describes the target values and success indicators. Section 3 provides the trend value of success indicators, and barring few exceptions, in most of the cases, the performance of the ministry is very good.

9   Between and within differences are studied through a statistical tool ANOVA. Some ministries are mostly dealing with organized sectors (such as finance, commerce, civil aviation, defence) and some with social issues (such as labour, social justice, rural development) where a large number of stakeholders and teething issues inhibit the achievement of government programmes. Hence, the degree performance by nature will differ from one ministry to another ministry ('between' difference). Similarly

within each ministry, some programmes are easy to implement and, hence, has a high degree of success. Does it mean 'within' a ministry government is indicating to differentiate officers without looking at the kind of projects in hand?

10 Refer to Report of Working Group on Tourism: XII Plan (2012–2017).

11 Read the article 'Caught in the Fire' by Padmaprana Ghosh, published in the Crest Edition, *The Times of India*, 25 August 2012.

12 For more understanding, you may refer to the article by Krithi K. Karanth and Ruth DeFries (2011) 'Nature-based tourism in Indian protected areas: New challenges for park management' published in *Conservation Letters*; volume 4, issue 2, 137–149, April/May 2011.

13 'Case Study on the Effects of Tourism on Culture and the Environment: India' (Jaisalmer, Khajuraho, and Goa); RACAP Series on Culture and Tourism in Asia, UNESCO, Bangkok.

14 Sejuti Jha (2011). 'Preferential Trade and Rules of Origin: A Study of India's Preferential Trading Arrangements', PhD thesis submitted at IIFT, New Delhi.

15 Deloitte–FICCI White Paper (2011). 'India ASEAN Free Trade Agreement: Implication for India's Economy'.

16 Sikdar, C. and B. Nag (2011). 'Impact of India ASEAN Free Trade Agreement: A Cross-country Analysis using Applied General Equilibrium Modeling', ARTNet Working Paper Series, No. 107, November.

17 http://www.indianhighcommission.com.my/market_survey.pdf accessed on 14 November 2012.

18 The cover story of the issue 11–17 May 2013.

19 For more discussion, refer to the book *Fighting Irrelevance: The Role of Regional Trade Agreements in International Production Networks in Asia*; UNESCAP, 2011, http://www.unescap.org/tid/publication/tipub2597.pdf.

20 Henry Chesbrough, Wim Vanhaverbeke, and Joel West (2006). *Open Innovation: Researching a New Paradigm* (Oxford University Press).

21 Integration Insight, Inspired by Grail Research, http://grailresearch.com/pdf/ContenPodsPdf/Grail-Research-The-Rising-Middle-Class-Africa.pdf.

22 http://www.bpart.kiev.ua/eng/cat2012/?s=3&i=476 accessed on 27 July 2014.

23 http://www.emory.edu/SOC/globalisation/debates.html

24 'Teaching Globalisation' by Muqtedar Khan, *Globalist,* 28 August 2003.

25 http://www.globalpolicy.org/globaliz/index.htm